SADDLEBACK
PUBLISHING·INC.

READING
FICTION 2

- **Drama**
- **Myths and Legends**
- **Folktales and Fables**
- **Popular Poetry**

READING
in context

READING in context

PRACTICAL READING 1

PRACTICAL READING 2

READING NONFICTION 1

READING NONFICTION 2

READING FICTION 1

READING FICTION 2

SADDLEBACK PUBLISHING·INC.

Three Watson
Irvine, CA 92618-2767

E-Mail: info@sdlback.com
Website: www.sdlback.com

Development and Production: Laurel Associates, Inc.
Cover Design: Elisa Ligon
Interior Illustrations: Ginger Slonaker

ISBN 1-56254-194-3

Printed in the United States of America
05 04 03 02 01   9 8 7 6 5 4 3 2 1

CONTENTS

INTRODUCTION

A NOTE TO THE STUDENT

Skillful readers have many advantages in life. While they are in school, they obviously get better grades. But the benefits go far beyond the classroom. Good readers are also good thinkers, problem-solvers, and decision-makers. They can avoid many of the problems and frustrations that unskilled readers miss out on. In short, good readers have a much greater chance to be happy and successful in all areas of their lives.

READING IN CONTEXT is an all-around skill-building program. Its purpose is to help you achieve your goals in life by making you a better reader. Each of the six worktexts has been designed with your needs and interests in mind. The reading selections are engaging and informative—some lighthearted and humorous, others quite serious and thought-provoking. The follow-up exercises teach the essential skills and concepts that lead to reading mastery.

We suggest that you thumb through the book before you begin work. Read the table of contents. Notice that each of the four units is based on a unifying theme. Then take a moment to look through the four lessons that make up each theme-based unit. Scan one of the *Before reading* paragraphs that introduces a lesson. Glance at the *Preview* and *Review* pages that begin and end each unit. "Surveying" this book (or any book) in this informal way is called *prereading*. It helps you "get a fix on" the task ahead by showing you how the book is organized. Recognizing patterns is an important thinking skill in itself. And in this case it will make you more comfortable and confident as you begin your work.

Happy reading!

PREVIEW

DRAMA

LESSON 1: Identifying Conflict: *Romeo and Juliet*

LESSON 2: Appreciating Historical Drama: *Julius Caesar*

LESSON 3: Creating Mood: *A Christmas Carol*

LESSON 4: Recognizing Plot Structure: *Antigone*

When you complete this unit, you will be able to answer questions like these:

- *What is the main conflict in* Romeo and Juliet*?*

- *What events from* Julius Caesar *are historical facts? What parts of the play come from the playwright's imagination?*

- *How do writers use words to create a mood?*

- *What is the main conflict in* Antigone, *and how is it resolved in the end?*

PRETEST

Write **T** or **F** to show whether you think each statement is *true* or *false*.

1. _____ A problem is a conflict between people, ideas, or forces.

2. _____ In fiction, problems are always happily resolved.

3. _____ Historical fiction and fantasy are both realistic stories that tell about true-life events.

4. _____ In order to be historical fiction, a story must only include events that actually happened and characters who really lived.

5. _____ The mood of a story is the feeling and atmosphere the words create.

6. _____ The main problem in a story is usually solved near the very end.

Pretest answers: 1. T 2. F 3. F 4. F 5. T 6. T

IDENTIFYING CONFLICT

Before reading . . .

Two young people meet at a party. From the moment they set eyes on each other, Romeo Montague and Juliet Capulet are in love. Will the deep, long-standing hatred between their powerful families keep them apart? To find out, read the abridged scene from Shakespeare's *Romeo and Juliet*.

ROMEO AND JULIET
Act II, Scene II

[Before dawn in the Capulets' walled garden in the town of Verona. A balcony of the Capulet mansion overlooks the garden. On the street side of the wall runs a narrow lane. Enter ROMEO in the lane. He climbs the wall into the garden. Moving in and out of the shadows, he approaches the Capulets' house. JULIET appears on the balcony of her second-floor room.]

ROMEO: But, soft, what light through yonder window breaks?
It is the east, and Juliet is the sun.
Arise fair sun, and kill the envious moon,
Who is already sick and pale with grief
That thou her maid are far more fair than she.
Her eye speaks to me. I will answer it.
I am too bold, 'tis not to me she speaks.
See how she leans her cheek upon her hand.
Oh, that I were a glove upon that hand,
That I might touch that cheek!

JULIET: Aye me!

ROMEO: She speaks! Oh, speak again, bright angel!

JULIET: *(not knowing Romeo is near and can hear her)*
O Romeo, Romeo, wherefore art thou Romeo?
Deny thy father and refuse thy name,
Or, if thou wilt not, be but sworn my love
And I'll no longer be a Capulet.

ROMEO: *(to himself)* Shall I hear more, or shall I speak at this?

JULIET: 'Tis but thy name that is my enemy.
Oh, be some other name. What's in a name?
That which we call a rose
By any other name would smell as sweet.
Romeo, put aside thy name
And for thy name which is no part of thee,
Take all myself!

ROMEO: *(speaking from the shadows)* I take thee at thy word!
Call me but love, and I'll take a new name.
Henceforth I never will be Romeo.

JULIET: *(startled)* What man art thou, that thus hidden in night
So stumblest on my secret thoughts?

ROMEO: By a name, I know how to tell thee who I am.
My name, dear saint, is hateful to myself
Because it is an enemy to thee.
Had I it written, I would tear the word.

JULIET: My ears have not yet drunk a hundred words
Of thy tongue's uttering, yet I know the sound.
Art thou not Romeo, and a Montague?

ROMEO: *(coming forward so that Juliet can see him)*
Neither, fair saint, if either thee dislike.

JULIET: If my kinsmen see thee, they will murder thee!

ROMEO: I have night's cloak to hide me from their eyes
If only thou love me, let them find me here.

JULIET: Dost thou love me? O gentle Romeo,
If thou dost love, say it faithfully.

ROMEO: Lady, by yonder blessed moon I swear,
That tips with silver all these fruit-tree tops—

JULIET: Oh, swear not by the moon, the inconstant moon,
That monthly changes in her circled orbit,
Lest that thy love prove likewise changeable.

[Juliet's nurse calls from inside the room.]

I hear some noise within; dear love, farewell.

[She calls to the nurse, then turns back to Romeo.]

In a moment, good Nurse.
Three words, dear Romeo, and good night indeed.

If that thy love be honorable,
Thy purpose marriage, send me word tomorrow
By someone I will get to come to thee,
Where and what time thou wilt perform the rite,
And all my fortunes at thy foot I'll lay
And follow thee my lord throughout the world.
Good night, good night. Parting is such sweet sorrow.
That I shall say good night till it be morrow.

[Juliet exits from the balcony.]

ROMEO: Sleep dwell upon thine eyes, peace in thy breast.
Would I were sleep and peace, so sweet to rest.

COMPREHENSION

Write your answers in complete sentences.

1. Why does Juliet feel free to declare her love for Romeo out loud?

   _____

2. Why is Romeo unwilling to tell Juliet his name?

   _____

3. Why is Juliet anxious for Romeo to leave the garden?

   _____

4. What does Juliet ask Romeo to do to prove his love is true?

   _____

UNDERSTANDING CHARACTER

What do we know about Romeo and Juliet from what they say and do in this scene?

1. Circle the *adjectives* that best describe the young lovers.

   impulsive   headstrong   practical   angry   obedient

   cautious   unemotional   romantic   timid   eager

2. Choose one of the adjectives you circled. Explain what Romeo and Juliet do and/or say to display this character trait.

_____

_____

VOCABULARY

Romeo and Juliet use words that are seldom heard in converstion today. Write a letter to match each word on the left with a more modern *synonym* (word that means the same). Hint: Find the word where it appears in the play. Context clues can help you figure out its meaning.

1. _____ **yonder**

2. _____ **'tis**

3. _____ **kinsmen**

4. _____ **thou**

5. _____ **dost**

6. _____ **thine**

a. does

b. you

c. it is (it's)

d. distant

e. relatives

f. your

PLOT: IDENTIFYING THE CONFLICT

The events of a plot always center around some type of problem or conflict. The conflict is usually introduced near the beginning. Throughout the story, events work toward a solution to the problem.

Read the following lines from *Romeo and Juliet*. Circle the letter of the speech that states the problem.

a. ROMEO: But, soft, what light through yonder window breaks?
     It is the east, and Juliet is the sun.

b. JULIET: 'Tis but thy name that is my enemy.
     Oh, be some other name.

c. JULIET: Good night, good night. Parting is such sweet sorrow.
     That I shall say good night till it be morrow.

9

USING STAGE DIRECTIONS

Playwrights usually provide set descriptions and directions for the actors. These directions often appear in italics or brackets. Reread the directions at the beginning of Act II, Scene II. List the most important props and set details. Then sketch a picture of the stage set in the box below.

SET DETAILS: _____

PARAPHRASING

When you *paraphrase*, you figure out the meaning of text and put it into your own words. On the lines provided, paraphrase each passage from Romeo and Juliet.

1. JULIET: Deny thy father and refuse thy name,
    Or, if thou wilt not, be but sworn my love
    And I'll no longer be a Capulet.

    PARAPHRASING: _____

    _____

2. ROMEO: Call me but love, and I'll take a new name.
    Henceforth I never will be Romeo.

    PARAPHRASING: _____

    _____

3. JULIET: What's in a name? That which we call a rose
    By any other name would smell as sweet.

    PARAPHRASING: _____

    _____

FIGURATIVE LANGUAGE

Circle a letter to show the meaning of the following lines:

1. *Arise fair sun, and kill the envious moon,*
   Who is already sick and pale with grief
   That thou her maid are far more fair than she.

   a. Romeo says the moon is jealous of Juliet because she is more beautiful than it is.

   b. Romeo says he is sick with love and only the light of the moon can cure him.

   c. Romeo wants the sun to come up and shine its light on Juliet's beautiful face.

2. *I have night's cloak to hide me from their eyes*
   If only thou love me, let them find me here.

   a. Romeo tells Juliet her love keeps him as warm and safe as a coat.

   b. Romeo means that it's cold out, and he wishes he had a cloak to wear.

   c. Romeo says that the darkness of night will hide him from Juliet's relatives.

3. *Oh, swear not by the moon, the inconstant moon,*
   That monthly changes in her circled orbit,
   Lest that thy love prove likewise changeable.

   a. Juliet worries that Romeo's love will change from day to day like the moon changes shape throughout the month.

   b. Juliet tells Romeo to watch his language and to be sure not to swear in front of her parents.

   c. Juliet says her love for Romeo is as bright as the light of the full moon.

APPRECIATING HISTORICAL DRAMA

Before reading . . .

It is 44 B.C. in Rome, Italy, and Julius Caesar has returned after leading a military victory. Most Romans cheer him. But some important citizens—those who have called themselves Caesar's friends—fear he is gaining too much power. They have plotted to stop him from making himself king. Caesar does not suspect their plot, but a soothsayer has foretold danger to Caesar on March 15, the ides of March. This adapted excerpt from William Shakespeare's Julius Caesar takes us to that fateful day.

JULIUS CAESAR

── CAST OF CHARACTERS ──	
Julius Caesar	*plotters against Caesar:*
Soothsayer	**Brutus** **Cassius**
Mark Anthony,	**Casca** **Cinna**
Caesar's supporter	**Trebonius**

Act III, Scene I

[In front of the Roman capital building. A horn blows. Caesar, Mark Anthony, Brutus, and Cassius enter stage left. A soothsayer enters from the right.]

CAESAR: *(to the soothsayer)* Ah, it is you! Well, the ides of March have come, old man. Where is the danger you predicted?

SOOTHSAYER: Beware, Caesar, but this day is not yet gone!

[Caesar pushes past the soothsayer and moves toward the capital. Brutus and Cassius speak together in hushed tones.]

BRUTUS: Does Caesar suspect our plot?

CASSIUS: We must go forward—but if our plans are discovered, I shall slay myself!

BRUTUS: Cassius, be calm. Look how Caesar smiles. He clearly suspects nothing.

CASSIUS: Yes, look you, Brutus. Our friend Trebonius draws Mark Anthony away from Caesar as planned.

[Trebonius and Casca move to the front of the crowd. Senators and citizens watch Caesar call the Roman Senate to order.]

CASSIUS: *(whispers to Brutus)* Casca will be first to raise his hand against Caesar.

CASCA: *(shouting)* Hands, speak for me!

[Casca rushes forward and stabs Caesar. Then the other plotters do the same, each man in turn.]

CAESAR: *(gasping for his last breath)* You too, Brutus? Are you against me also? Then fall Caesar! *(He dies.)*

CINNA: Liberty! Freedom! Tyranny is dead! Run hence, cry it about the streets!

CASSIUS: Tell the people! Speak of liberty and freedom!

BRUTUS: *(calling out to the fleeing crowd)* People and senators, do not be afraid. Fly not; stand still. We mean only to put an end to one man's ambition!

CASSIUS: Where is Mark Anthony?

TREBONIUS: Fled to his house, confused. Everywhere people are running about, crying wildly. They act as if doomsday has come.

BRUTUS: But Caesar's death was a sacrifice, not a murder! We have saved him twenty years of fearing death. Come, Romans! Let us bathe our hands and swords in Caesar's blood. Let us wave our red weapons over our heads. Let us all cry, "Peace, freedom, and liberty!" We must calm the fears of the people. *(Anthony enters and looks at Caesar's body.)* Welcome, Mark Anthony.

ANTHONY: I do not know your plans, but I know you are wise men. You will give me good reasons why Caesar had to die. All I seek is to take Caesar's body to the marketplace. I will speak there as his friend at a funeral.

BRUTUS: You shall, Mark Anthony. But I will speak first. I will explain why I—who honored Caesar—had to strike him down.

CASSIUS: Brutus, a word with you! *(He takes Brutus aside.)* You know not what you do! Do not let Anthony speak! Who knows what he will say to the people? I like this not!

[Everyone except Mark Anthony exits. Left alone with Caesar's body, Anthony speaks to his fallen friend.]

ANTHONY: *(kneeling beside the body)* Oh, dead Caesar, forgive me for being meek and gentle with these butchers! They have killed the noblest man who ever lived! Woe to those who shed your blood! I will avenge you!

COMPREHENSION

Write **T** or **F** on the line to show whether each statement is *true* or *false*.

1. _____ Brutus, Cassius, Casca, Trebonius, Cinna, and Mark Anthony were all involved in a plot to murder Caesar.

2. _____ Brutus had been a good friend of Caesar's.

3. _____ Caesar had been warned to be careful on this day.

4. _____ Brutus thought Caesar was a weak ruler.

5. _____ The plotters planned to kill Caesar in order to keep Rome free.

6. _____ Only Casca actually stabbed Caesar.

7. _____ Brutus agreed that Mark Anthony could speak at Caesar's funeral.

8. _____ Cassius thought it was a good idea for Anthony to speak at the funeral.

UNDERSTANDING THE TIMES

By reading the drama *Julius Caesar*, we can better understand this period in history. Think about the events in the scene. Then write **T** or **F** on the line to show whether each statement below is *true* or *false*.

1. _____ Some ancient Romans believed in superstitions and fortune telling.

2. _____ Julius Caesar was an unpopular man whom most Romans hated.

3. _____ Military glories were important in the eyes of the Roman people.

4. ____ It was against the law to carry weapons in the streets of Rome.

5. ____ Rulers and leaders remained in their castles and never appeared before the people.

APPRECIATING HISTORICAL DRAMA

Historical fiction combines imagination and fact. Both real and fictional characters are placed in a historically accurate setting to act out a story. Read the following paragraph about the real Julius Caesar.

> The Roman people honored Caesar for his leadership and military glories. His portrait was stamped on Roman coins. At a public festival, Mark Anthony offered Caesar the crown of king. Caesar refused it. Even so, important leaders suspected Caesar intended to make himself king. Marcus Brutus and Gaius Cassius led a plot to kill Caesar. On March 15, 44 B.C., Caesar was stabbed to death at a senate meeting. He received more than 20 wounds from the daggers of men who he had believed were his friends.

While the events of the play are historical fact, the words that Shakespeare's characters speak are fiction. Copy words from the play as directed below.

1. Copy words from the play that dramatize the stabbing of Julius Caesar. _____

   _____

2. Copy words from the play that show that Caesar and his murderers had been friends. _____

   _____

   _____

3. Copy words from the play that show that Brutus thought he was doing the best thing for Rome by killing Caesar. _____

   _____

   _____

VOCABULARY PUZZLER

Fill in the blanks with words from the box that match each definition.
Then write the circled letters in order on the lines at the bottom to complete
the sentence.

doomsday	soothsayer	suspect	senators	tyranny

1. one who sees the future;
   a fortune teller

   __ __ __ __ __ __ __ ◯ __ __

2. members of a group of leaders who
   help make government decisions

   __ __ __ __ __ ◯ __ __

3. to think of as guilty of some wrongdoing

   __ ◯ __ __ __ __ __

4. harsh and unjust government; unfair
   use of power

   ◯ __ __ __ __ __ __

5. the end of the world when people
   will face their final judgment

   __ ◯ ◯ __ __ __ __ __

Caesar's last words to Brutus were

"__ __ __ __ __ __, Brutus?"

SYNONYMS

Synonyms are words that have the same or nearly the same meaning. In each
group, circle the synonym of the **boldface** word from the play.

1. **plot**   celebration   conspiracy   practice   contest

2. **ambition**   desire   wealth   illness   fear

3. **funeral**   crowning   election   burial   meeting

4. **soothsayer** king   senator   friend   prophet

5. **confused**   happy   bewildered   angry   powerful

6. **slay**   murder   elect   fear   admire

SEQUENCE OF EVENTS

The following events of the play are listed out of order. Write the letters of the events on the lines in the box to show which happened first, second, and so on.

1. _____   2. _____   3. _____   4. _____   5. _____   6. _____   7. _____

   a. All the plotters stab Caesar.

   b. A soothsayer warns Caesar that the ides of March are not over.

   c. Cassius worries that Caesar suspects there is a plot against him.

   d. Brutus agrees to let Mark Anthony speak at Caesar's funeral.

   e. Caesar dies.

   f. Casca stabs Caesar.

   g. Caesar cries, "You too, Brutus?"

MAKING PREDICTIONS

Reread Mark Anthony's lines at the end of the scene. What do you predict will happen later in the play? Circle a letter to show your answer.

   a. A time of peace and democracy will come to Rome.

   b. Rome will face a time of trouble and unrest.

   c. Mark Anthony will offer Brutus the crown.

   d. Mark Anthony will forgive Caesar's killers and work with them in government.

CREATING MOOD

Before reading . . .

Ebenezer Scrooge knows how to make plenty of money. What he doesn't know is how to enjoy his life and appreciate the people in it. Then, one Christmas Eve, a dead business partner and three other ghosts come to call. Their visits open Scrooge's eyes and make him a different man. The following scene is a dramatic adaptation of Charles Dickens's *A Christmas Carol.*

A CHRISTMAS CAROL

[Christmas Eve, London, England. Ebenezer Scrooge's gloomy bedroom is lit by a single candle. There is a curtained bed, one table, and a chair. A small fire burns in a stove. Scrooge dozes before the fire. A bell tolls.]

SCROOGE: (*waking*) What's that? There's no bell in my house. (*Now there are sounds of metal scraping against wood.*) And *that*? What's that sound? It's like chains dragging across the floor. It's like the sound of a ghost. (*Scrooge shakes his head.*) Ghosts! Humbug! There are no ghosts!

[Lights flash. A figure enters. A chain is wrapped around the visitor like a belt. It drags on the floor and is made partly of cashboxes, keys, and padlocks.]

MARLEY: (*in a mournful, quivering voice*) Ebenezer Scrooge!

SCROOGE: (*amazed*) Who are you?

MARLEY: Better to ask me who I was. In life I was your partner at the counting-house, Jacob Marley. But I see you don't believe in me.

SCROOGE: Surely you are the unfortunate result of some bad beef, an underdone potato, or too much gravy that I ate this evening. There *are* no ghosts! Humbug, I tell you. Ghosts are humbug!

MARLEY: (*shrieking and shaking his chains*) Look closely at me, Scrooge! Take note of my chains. I made them myself during my life. Business and money—that's all I ever cared for. I never shared what I had. I never thought of others. You are the same, Scrooge, and you have such a chain yourself. Yours is far heavier than mine by now. I must walk the earth wearing these chains and regretting things I might have done while I was alive. *Take warning, Ebenezer.* This is a preview of what will happen to you!

SCROOGE: (*looking frightened and falling to his knees*) Is there no hope for me, Jacob? Speak to me! Give me hope!

MARLEY: I have none to give. I cannot stay any longer. (*Shrieking again and shaking his chains*) Oh, it is at Christmas time that I suffer most. I see others sharing joy that I never shared. Hear me now! My time is nearly gone. I have come to warn you that you have yet a chance of escaping my fate.

SCROOGE: You always were a good friend to me, Jacob. Tell me how.

MARLEY: You will be haunted by three spirits.

SCROOGE: (*shivering*) I think I'd rather not.

MARLEY: Without their visits, you cannot hope to avoid the path I've taken. Expect the first one—the Ghost of Christmas Past—when the clock chimes one. Your next visitor will be the Ghost of Christmas Present. The third and final guest will be the Ghost of Christmas Yet to Come. Now, you will see me no more. For your own sake, don't fail to recall what has passed between us!

[The bedroom window opens on its own. Sad, wailing sounds come into the room with the wind. Marley's ghost disappears through the window.]

SCROOGE: (*crossing to the window and closing it*) Hum . . .

[Scrooge cannot finish the word *humbug*. He goes to his bed and pulls the covers up over his head. He sleeps for a moment. Then he is wakened by a clock chiming the hour of one. There is the sound of something moving across the floor. Lights flash and a mysterious figure pulls back Scrooge's covers.]

SCROOGE: Are you the spirit whose coming was foretold to me?

GHOST: I am! I am the Ghost of Christmas Past—your past. (*taking Scrooge by the arm*) Rise and walk with me!

COMPREHENSION

Circle the letter of the words that best complete each statement.

1. Marley's ghost visits Scrooge in order to

   a. warn Scrooge that he should change his ways.

   b. bring Scrooge a lovely Christmas gift.

   c. warn Scrooge his clerk is stealing money.

   d. suggest that Scrooge work harder.

2. Early in the scene, Scrooge

   a. believes in ghosts.

   b. does not believe in ghosts.

   c. is a ghost himself.

   d. is scared to death of ghosts.

3. The chains on Marley's ghost suggest that in life he was

   a. friendly and outgoing.

   b. greedy and miserly.

   c. fun-loving and wild.

   d. giving and generous.

4. Marley's ghost tells Scrooge he should expect to

   a. die very soon.

   b. have a merry Christmas.

   c. have three ghostly visitors.

   d. make lots of money.

5. At the end of the scene, Scrooge is visited by

   a. his clerk from the counting-house.

   b. his landlord asking for rent money.

   c. a ghost who will show him Christmases of the future.

   d. a ghost who will show him Christmases from his past.

PREFIXES

Add a prefix from the box to each word in parentheses. Write the new word on the line to complete each sentence.

pre-	under-	fore-	re-	dis-	un-

1. "Look at me, Scrooge," Marley said. "I am a **(view)** _____

   of what will happen to you."

2. Marley **(told)** _____ Ebenezer Scrooge's miserable future.

3. Scrooge thought the ghostly vision was a nightmare—the
   (fortunate) _____ result of a bad dinner.

4. He was sure the beef had been taken from the oven too soon
   and was **(done)** _____.

5. The Ghost of Christmas Past came to help Scrooge **(call)**
   _____ holidays from his childhood.

6. As quickly as Marley appeared in the room, he **(appeared)**
   _____ out the window and was gone.

RECOGNIZING CAUSE AND EFFECT

Think about the events in the scene. *Why* do the events occur, and *what* happens
as a result? Complete the following chart by writing the missing *cause* or *effect* on
the blank lines.

| CAUSE | → | EFFECT |

CAUSE	EFFECT
1. Because _____ _____	Jacob Marley visits Scrooge.
2. Because _____ _____	Scrooge begins to believe in ghosts.
3. Because Marley was such a money-loving miser in life,	he _____ _____

RECOGNIZING REALISTIC FICTION AND FANTASY

Both realistic fiction and fantasies are created in the author's imagination. A *realistic story* tells about something that **could** happen. A *fantasy* is a story about something that **could not** happen.

Answers the questions on the lines.

1. Is *A Christmas Carol* a realistic story or a fantasy? _____

2. What events from this scene led you to your conclusion?

   _____

   _____

CREATING MOOD

The feeling or atmosphere of a story is its *mood*. Authors must choose words carefully to create a certain mood.

Notice the **boldface** words in the following sentences from *A Christmas Carol*. Write the word and its meaning on the line. If you need help, use context clues or a dictionary. Then use at least three of the words in a descriptive paragraph. Try to create a scary mood as you describe a real or imagined place.

1. *Ebenezer Scrooge's* **gloomy** *bedroom is lit by a single candle.*

   _____ : _____

2. *(in a* **mournful***, quivering voice) Ebenezer Scrooge!*

   _____ : _____

3. **MARLEY:** *(***shrieking** *and shaking his chains) Look closely at me, Scrooge.*

   _____ : _____

4. *Sad,* **wailing** *sounds come into the room with the wind.*

   _____ : _____

5. *Lights flash and a* **mysterious** *figure pulls back Scrooge's covers.*

   _____ : _____

Your descriptive paragraph:

_____

_____

_____

_____

_____

_____

_____

_____

SYNONYM PUZZLER

Synonyms are words that have nearly the same meanings. Match each clue word with a vocabulary word (its synonym) from the box. Write the vocabulary word on the crossword puzzle. Use a dictionary if you need help.

chimes	**fate**	**ghost**	**humbug**
regretting	**share**	**counting-house**	

ACROSS

3. Phooey!

5. destiny

6. spirit

7. business office

DOWN

1. bemoaning

2. give

4. rings

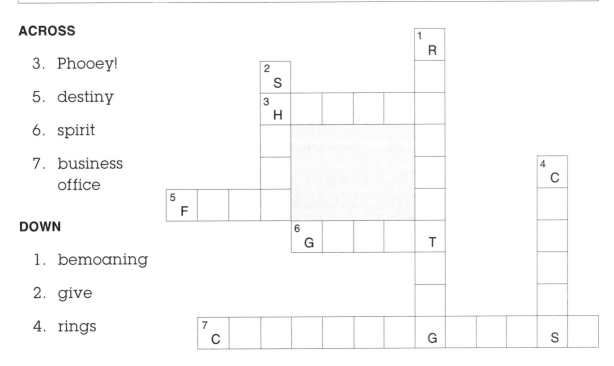

Before reading . . .

In the fifth century B.C., the playwright Sophocles wrote a tragic play based on a Greek legend. Audiences gathered to watch masked actors present scenes filled with action and color. In this short, adapted scene from the play, you'll meet Antigone, the title character. She is the proud daughter of the late king of Thebes. You'll also meet Creon, her uncle and the present king. When Antigone ignores the king's decree, she faces harsh consequences.

ANTIGONE

CAST OF CHARACTERS	
Chorus	Haemon, *King Creon's son, engaged to marry Antigone*
Antigone	
Ismene, *Antigone's sister*	First and Second Guards
Creon, *King of Thebes*	Teiresias, *a prophet*

[SCENE: In front of the palace at Thebes. It is the morning after Antigone's two brothers have died in battle. Antigone talks with her sister Ismene.]

ANTIGONE: Sister, our family has seen bad times. The gods have not been kind. And now there is the new decree Creon has ordered. Have you heard?

ISMENE: I know only that our brothers have died. What more is there?

ANTIGONE: Creon has allowed one brother, Eteocles, to be properly buried. But Polyneices—who dared to stand against Creon—will not have a burial. His body will be left for birds to feast upon. Will you help me bury our brother?

ISMENE: (*frightened*) You would bury him when it is forbidden? Think, sister! We two are alone in the world now. We cannot go against a king's decree!

ANTIGONE: I will not force you to help me. But I *shall* bury my brother!

[Exit Antigone and Ismene.]

CHORUS: Once Creon was a happy man, but the duties of king have weighed heavily on him. Now he rules without mercy or kindness.

[Creon and a guard enter.]

FIRST GUARD: The body of Polyneices is gone! Someone must have buried it!

CREON: Whoever has done this deed shall pay with his life!

[A second guard enters, bringing Antigone.]

SECOND GUARD: We caught this girl burying Polyneices. She was crying over his grave. We rushed forward and seized her.

CREON: (*to Antigone*) Do you deny this?

ANTIGONE: I do not. Do with me what you will. I could not leave my brother to lie unburied.

CHORUS: Antigone is a brave and passionate girl.

CREON: You have defied the king! No matter that you are my sister's child. No matter that you were to marry my son! You must be punished!

[The guards drag Antigone away.]

CHORUS: The angry king feels that Antigone has mocked his power.

[Haemon enters.]

HAEMON: Father, I have heard of Antigone's deed. You are king, and I honor you. But surely you will put family before all else. I ask you to do what is *right*—nothing more. If Antigone dies, there is another who will die with her. [Haemon exits.]

CHORUS: Though his son pleads for Antigone's release, Creon will not be moved.

CREON: I will not show weakness toward those who defy my laws! Antigone shall be locked away in a cave. Whatever the fates decide shall come to her. [Creon exits.]

CHORUS: Antigone is left in her lonely prison. The blind prophet Teiresias brings Creon a warning.

[Creon enters in front of the palace. Teiresias follows, tapping with a cane.]

CREON: Aged Teiresias! What words do you bring?

TEIRESIAS: Listen! All humans make mistakes. But they must be put right. The gods are displeased with your actions. Your house shall be filled with wailing and grief.

[Exit Creon and Teiresias.]

CHORUS: The prophet's words frighten the king. He goes to undo what he has done. But it is too late! Rather than go on living as a prisoner, Antigone has hung herself. Haemon, grieving over his lost bride, drives his sword into his own chest. And the gods are not yet finished with Creon. Returning to the palace, he finds that his wife has died from sorrow.

[Enter Creon before the palace.]

CREON: I—I have killed my son and my wife, too. (*He staggers into the palace.*)

CHORUS: A sad and gloomy peace settles over Thebes. The king is left alone. Now he has nothing to do but issue orders and wait for his own death.

COMPREHENSION

Circle a letter to show the best ending for each sentence.

1. The purpose of the Chorus is to

   a. help Antigone bury Polyneices.

   b. comment on the characters' actions.

   c. teach Creon a lesson.

   d. act as a third guard.

2. The main conflict of the story is between

   a. Antigone and Creon.

   b. Antigone and Haemon.

   c. the Chorus and Creon.

   d. Antigone and Ismene.

3. Antigone is upset because

   a. Haemon is going to marry another woman.

   b. her father is dead.

   c. her brother will not get a proper burial.

   d. Creon is a bad king.

4. Antigone dies as the result of

   a. starvation.

   b. loneliness.

   c. hanging herself.

   d. being hung by Creon.

5. Creon loses

   a. his son.   b. his wife.   c. his niece.   d. all three.

RECOGNIZING PLOT STRUCTURE

A story plot has a beginning, middle, and end. Events early in the story set up the problem. In the middle, events move the story forward. Events at the end of the story solve the problem.

Write two events from *Antigone* that belong in each stage of the plot.

BEGINNING: _____

_____

MIDDLE: _____

_____

END: _____

_____

IDIOMS

The following lines contain *idioms*—expressions that have a meaning beyond the words' usual definitions. Circle a letter to show the meaning of the **boldface** expression in each sentence.

1. Once Creon was a good, happy man. But the duties of king have **weighed heavily on him**.

   a. He has gained weight while acting as king.

   b. Being king has caused him a lot of stress.

   c. The crown of Thebes is very heavy.

2. Whoever has done this deed shall **pay a heavy price**!

   a. Criminals in Thebes are fined a lot of money.

   b. Citizens of Thebes pay high taxes.

   c. The punishment for the crime will be severe.

3. Though his son pleads for Antigone's release, Creon **will not be moved**.

   a. Creon is stiff and old and has trouble moving about.

   b. Nothing can get Creon to change his mind.

   c. Creon never leaves the palace grounds.

IDENTIFYING CHARACTERS

Write a letter on the line to match each character with his or her role.

1. _____ **Antigone**   a. the king of Thebes

2. _____ **Creon**   b. daughter of a past king, the heroine of the play

3. _____ **Haemon**   c. a blind prophet of Thebes

4. _____ **Ismene**   d. Antigone's sister

5. _____ **Teiresias**   e. son of Creon, engaged to Antigone

UNDERSTANDING CHARACTERS

Read the following lines from the play. Circle the word or words that best complete each statement. Then write a word of your own that could also describe the character.

1. **ISMENE:** You would bury him when it is forbidden? Think, sister! We two are alone now. We cannot go against a king's decree!

   THESE LINES SHOW THAT ISMENE IS: bold   fearful   stupid   angry

   ANOTHER DESCRIPTIVE WORD: _____

2. **ANTIGONE:** Do with me what you will. I could not leave my brother to lie unburied.

   THESE LINES SHOW THAT ANTIGONE IS: bold   fearful   stupid   bossy

   ANOTHER DESCRIPTIVE WORD: _____

3. **CREON:** You have defied the king! No matter that you are to marry my son! You must be punished.

   THESE LINES SHOW THAT CREON IS: weak   proud   forgiving   loving

   ANOTHER DESCRIPTIVE WORD: _____

VOCABULARY

Write words from the box to complete the following paragraph. Use the definitions in parentheses as clues.

burial	**decree**	**defied**	**grief**	**mocked**	**passionate**

King Creon would not allow Antigone's brother to have

a proper _____ (1. the act of putting something in

the ground). He issued a _____ (2. ruling, order)

saying anyone who tried to bury Polyneices would be punished.

Antigone was _____ (3. feeling very strongly) about

family loyalty. She _____ (4. opposed, went against)

Creon's order. Proud King Creon felt that Antigone's actions

_____ (5. made fun of, scoffed) his authority.

He punished her harshly, but this harsh decision brought him

much _____ (6. sorrow, sadness).

POINT OF VIEW

Imagine that you are each character. Write two or three sentences explaining the problem of the story from *your* point of view.

1. **Antigone:** _____

    _____

    _____

    _____

2. **Creon:** _____

    _____

    _____

    _____

REVIEW

MATCHING

Write a letter to match each play with its main conflict.

1. _____ **Romeo and Juliet**

2. _____ **Julius Caesar**

3. _____ **A Christmas Carol**

4. _____ **Antigone**

a. Rebels feel they must stop a leader from gaining too much power.

b. A miserly man is letting greed and selfishness destroy him.

c. A lone young woman stands up against a powerful king.

d. Two young people fall in love, but their families forbid their marriage.

COMPREHENSION

Write your answers in your own words.

1. How are the personalities of Juliet Capulet and Antigone alike?

_____

_____

2. Caesar says "You too, Brutus?" before he dies. Why is he surprised to see that Brutus is one of his murderers?

_____

_____

3. How is the mood of *A Christmas Carol* different from the mood of most holiday stories?

_____

_____

4. What clues do you have that *A Christmas Carol* takes place in a past time rather than in modern-day London?

_____

_____

MYTHS AND LEGENDS

LESSON 1: Understanding Characters: *Wings: The Myth of Daedalus and Icarus*

LESSON 2: Identifying Setting: *How the Winds Began to Blow*

LESSON 3: Drawing Conclusions: *Odin's Quest for Wisdom*

LESSON 4: Putting Events in Order: *The Sword in the Stone*

When you complete this unit, you will be able to answer questions like these:

- *How do a character's words and actions reveal personality?*

- *How might a change in setting affect the events of a story?*

- *How do readers form opinions about characters and events? How can they tell if their conclusions make sense?*

- *How can recognizing the sequence of events help a reader understand a story better?*

PRETEST

Write **T** or **F** to show whether you think each statement is *true* or *false*.

1. _____ Readers can understand a character better by reflecting on that character's actions.

2. _____ The words that characters speak seldom tell anything about their personalities.

3. _____ Authors always tell exactly where and when the story takes place.

4. _____ You can use clues such as weather, clothing, and speech patterns to figure out where and when a story takes place.

5. _____ A conclusion is a sensible decision that a reader reaches by thinking about facts and details.

6. _____ Events presented *in sequence* are told in the order of time.

UNDERSTANDING CHARACTERS

Before reading . . .

Have you ever thought how exciting it would be to soar like a bird? In this myth, Daedalus gives his son Icarus just that chance. But as he took off, the boy forgot he was a mere human. Icarus flew—but he paid a heavy price!

WINGS: THE MYTH OF DAEDALUS AND ICARUS

Long ago, on the island of Crete, lived a clever inventor named Daedalus. He was known throughout Greece as a builder of amazing things. King Minos was the ruler of Crete. He ordered Daedalus to build a huge maze with thousands of twists and turns. Minos used this labyrinth as a prison for captured enemies.

When a soldier of Athens escaped from the maze, Minos suspected that Daedalus had helped the prisoner! The king found a way to punish the builder and keep him from using his skills in other kingdoms. He imprisoned Daedalus and his son Icarus in the maze. Poor Daedalus could not find his way out of the snaking paths of his own creation!

"We shall die here!" cried young Icarus. "Even if we escape from the maze, King Minos will never allow a ship to carry us to freedom."

But Daedalus had an inventor's spirit. As he watched the seagulls soaring overhead, he got an idea. "Escape may be checked by water and land," he declared, "but the air and the sky are free!"

Daedalus began trapping seagulls. He plucked their feathers and mounded the plumage into piles. After studying the gull's bone structure, he built a framework of twigs. Using candle wax, he glued feathers to the frames. At last Daedalus had built wings big enough to carry a man. Then he made a smaller pair—just right for Icarus.

As Daedalus strapped the wings to his son, the boy could not stand still. He was *too* eager to fly! Daedalus worried. He knew his son could be more fearless than wise. "Be still, Icarus, and listen," Daedalus said. "You must stay near me. Do not fly too close to the sea. Your wings could get wet and drag you down. And beware of flying too high— or the sun will melt the wax. *Keep a middle course!*" Daedalus warned. "That is the way to stay safe."

When both sets of wings were in place, a breeze was blowing. Daedalus and Icarus flapped their arms. Soon the wind lifted them from their prison.

As long as Icarus stayed close to Daedalus, the pair flew steadily toward the mainland. But—as often happens— the youth forgot his elder's advice. Icarus grew impatient. "Father is too old to enjoy this!" he cried. He flew higher.

"Come back!" Daedalus shouted.

Did Icarus ignore the shouts? Did the wind snatch the words away? No one knows. But we do know the boy flew up toward the sun. Daedalus tried to follow—but it was too late. The sun had melted the wax. Icarus's wings were falling apart! Icarus flapped wildly, but he no longer had the wings of a bird—just human arms. Daedalus was horrified. He could do nothing but watch the fall. He circled for hours, but the sea had swallowed his boy.

Finally, Daedalus flew on. At last the sobbing father reached the mainland. There he stripped off his wings and hid them where they would never be found. The power of flight, Daedalus decided, was best left to birds and gods.

COMPREHENSION

Write your answers in complete sentences.

1. What were two reasons that King Minos imprisoned Daedalus?

   _____

   _____

2. What gave Daedalus the idea of a way to get off the island?

   _____

   _____

3. Why did Icarus fall into the sea?

   _____

   _____

UNDERSTANDING CHARACTERS

Remember that both actions and words reveal things about a character's personality.

1. Read the character traits in the box. Then list each trait under the character it describes.

youthful	skillful	cautious	excitable	careless
reckless	clever	observant	adventurous	sensible

   DAEDALUS   **ICARUS**

   _____   _____

   _____   _____

   _____   _____

   _____   _____

2. Write one trait you listed under *Daedalus*. _____

   What does Daedalus *do* that shows this trait?_____

   _____

   What does Daedalus *say* that shows this trait?_____

   _____

3. Write one trait you listed under *Icarus*. _____

   What does Icarus *do* that shows this trait? _____

   _____

   What does Icarus *say* that shows this trait? _____

   _____

4. What thought does Daedalus have about Icarus that says

   something about the boy's character? _____

   _____

USING SYNONYMS AS CONTEXT CLUES

Synonyms (words with similar meanings) can help a reader figure out unfamiliar words. Read the following sentences from the myth. In each sentence or pair of sentences, find and circle a synonym for the **boldface** word.

1. Long ago, on the island of Crete, lived a clever **inventor** named Daedalus. He was known throughout Greece as a builder of amazing things.

2. King Minos, the ruler of Crete, ordered Daedalus to build a huge **maze** with thousands of twists and turns. Minos used this labyrinth as a prison for captured enemies.

3. He plucked their **feathers** and mounded the plumage into piles.

4. Daedalus had studied the gull's bone **structure**. Now he built a framework of twigs.

PUZZLER

First, unscramble each group of letters to make a word. Then combine the unscrambled words to make *compound words* found in the myth. (A compound word is made up of two or more word parts. Each part can stand alone as a word.) Finally, use one of the compound words to complete sentences 9–12.

1. **ase** _____

2. **nami** _____

3. **rfmae** _____

4. **deah** _____

5. **oevr** _____

6. **dlna** _____

7. **sllug** _____

8. **kowr** _____

9. Daedalus watched birds flying _____.

10. Daedalus and Icarus plucked feathers from _____.

11. Daedalus made a twig _____ to hold the feathers.

12. The father and son planned to escape to the _____.

UNDERSTANDING THE TIMES

The myth of Daedalus and Icarus helps us understand the ancient Greeks. Think about the story events. Then write **T** or **F** to show whether you think each of the following statements is *true* or *false*.

1. _____ The ancient Greeks worshipped many gods.

2. _____ Ancient Greece was governed by strong rulers.

3. _____ Greek kings always governed wisely and fairly.

4. _____ There were no wars in ancient Greece.

5. _____ Kids in ancient Greece always listened to their elders.

DRAWING CONCLUSIONS

Circle the letter of the best answer to each question.

1. Why do you think Daedalus carefully warned Icarus to stay close?

   a. There were flying monsters in the skies.
   b. Daedalus was frightened and wanted company.
   c. Daedalus knew his son was young and reckless.

2. Why do you think Icarus ignored his father and flew higher?

   a. Icarus got carried away with excitement.
   b. Icarus did not think his father knew very much.
   c. Icarus knew a quicker way to the mainland.

3. What did Daedalus think was the best way to stay safe in life?

   a. to be daring and adventurous at all times
   b. to take the middle path and avoid extremes
   c. to be very cautious and stay at home

4. After Icarus drowned, what conclusion did Daedalus reach?

   a. He should not use wax as a glue.
   b. People were not meant to fly.
   c. He should have obeyed King Minos.

VOCABULARY

Choose the vocabulary word from the box that best completes each word group.

desperate	ignore	inventor	maze	soar	youth

1. fly, rise, _____

2. puzzle, web, _____

3. disregard, overlook, _____

4. youngster, adolescent, _____

5. designer, engineer, _____

6. frantic, hopeless, _____

IDENTIFYING SETTING

Before reading...

This Eskimo myth tells a happy story. It also explains, as myths often do, the way things work in the natural world. Read on to meet a lonely couple whose dreams come true.

HOW THE WINDS BEGAN TO BLOW

The Wish

When the world was new, a loving couple lived in a village near the mouth of the Yukon River. Their world was very quiet and calm. This place was peaceful because there were no winds—none at all. Snow never drifted here. Leaves never rustled on the trees.

Although the couple enjoyed life beside the cold river, something was missing. Every evening, they wished for a son or daughter to share their fire.

The Dream

One night the woman dreamed of a sled glowing in the moonlight. A mysterious driver, cloaked in fur, beckoned to her. When she climbed in, the sled rose into the icy air. It was then the woman recognized the driver. He was Igaluk, the Moon Spirit, who brought good fortune.

The sled descended into an ice field where a lone tree stood. Igaluk said, "If you make a doll from this tree trunk, your wish will come true."

When the woman woke, she roused her husband and described her dream. "Please find the tree!" she cried.

Grumbling, the husband shouldered his ax and went into the frosty night. He'd not gone far when he saw a moonbeam lighting a silver path in the snow. The man followed it to a single tree that glowed like a star. Surely this was the tree from the dream! He cut it and carried it home.

In the morning, the man carved the figure of a boy from the wood. His wife sewed a tiny sealskin suit. But by bedtime, the figure still remained lifeless. The couple felt gloomy and quite ridiculous. That night, however, a sound woke them. Something was moving inside their hut.

"It's the doll!" cried the wife. Sure enough, the figure was alive! The couple hugged and cuddled it until they happily fell back to sleep.

"Wake up, son!" cried the woman the next morning. But to the couple's sorrow, the doll was nowhere to be found!

The Winds

The living doll had gone outside to explore the world. He followed the moonbeam path to the place where a wall separated the Land of Earth from the Land of Sky. There was a hole in the wall covered by a flap of animal skin. The curious doll pulled the cover aside.

Whoosh! A strong wind rushed in from the Land of Sky. It carried all types of birds. For a while, the doll enjoyed the breezes and the singing birds. But then he pulled the skin back over the hole. He said sternly, "Wind, blow hard sometimes. Blow softly sometimes. And sometimes, don't blow at all."

Suddenly, the doll remembered the kind couple back home. He felt he'd seen enough of the world. By the time the doll arrived at the hut, winds had begun to blow. From that time on, some days they blew hard. Some days they blew softly. And some days they were still. People were pleased—for the winds brought birds of all kinds and good hunting too. The couple held a feast to thank Igaluk, the Moon Spirit. Now people everywhere make dolls to bring happiness to their own children.

COMPREHENSION

Write **T** if the statement is *true* and **F** if the statement is *false*.

1. _____ The couple wished for good hunting and wealth.

2. _____ The woman was frightened of Igaluk, the Moon Spirit.

3. _____ The woman believed that her dream showed her a way to have a child.

4. _____ The couple found the doll by the riverbank.

5. _____ The doll was carved from the bark of a magic tree.

6. _____ The doll did not like the couple, so he ran away.

7. _____ The doll very much wanted to see the world.

8. _____ Because the doll was evil, he let harsh winds into the world.

9. _____ After the doll removed the wind flap, it was windy all the time.

10. _____ The people were pleased with the new winds.

IDENTIFYING SETTING

The place and time of a story can influence the actions of the characters and the events. Think about how setting affects what happens in "How the Winds Began to Blow." Then circle the letter of the correct answer.

1. Where does this story take place?

   a. in the Land of Sky

   b. along the banks of the Yukon River

   c. in a tropical land

2. When does this story take place?

   a. in the present

   b. in the distant past

   c. far in the future

40

3. Complete the *setting web* below. In the outer circles, copy words and phrases from the myth that helped you identify and picture the setting.

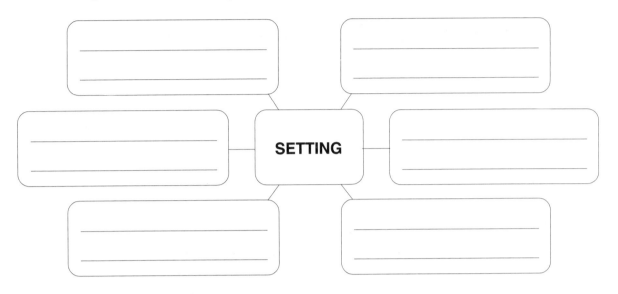

4. How do you think this story would be different if it were set in the present day?

_____

_____

_____

_____

VOCABULARY: MULTIPLE MEANINGS

Many words have more than one meaning, depending on how they are used in a sentence. Read the following sentences and think about the meaning of the **boldface** word. Circle the letter of the word meaning used in the sentence.

1. Long ago, when the world was new, a loving couple lived in a village near the **mouth** of the Yukon River.

   a. opening in the head through which food is taken in

   b. opening in a river where water empties into another body of water

2. Snow never **drifted**.

    a. piled in heaps from the force of the wind   b. got carried along by a current of water

3. Leaves never **rustled** on the trees.

    a. stole cattle or horses   b. made soft, rubbing sounds

4. Then the woman knew the driver was Igaluk, the Moon Spirit, who brought good **fortune**.

    a. a large sum of money   b. future events; those yet to happen

5. He **shouldered** his ax and marched into the frosty night.

    a. to put or carry on one's shoulder   b. to take on the responsibility for

6. His wife sewed a little sealskin suit for the **figure**.

    a. the symbol of a number   b. a shape or form

SUFFIXES

Some of the story words have *suffixes*—word parts added to the end of base words. Notice that suffixes can change a word's part of speech.

    EXAMPLE: happy (adjective) + -ly = happily (adverb)

Add a suffix from the box to each word below. Make sure the new word is a different part of speech

-ly	-y	-ous	-ness

1. **gloom** (noun) + _____ = _____ (adjective)

2. **mystery** (noun) + _____ = _____ (adjective)

3. **stern** (adjective) + _____ = _____ (adverb)

4. **soft** (adjective) + _____ = _____ (adverb)

5. **calm** (adjective) + _____ = _____ (noun)

6. **love** (noun) + _____ = _____ (adjective)

7. **happy** (adjective) + _____ = _____ (noun)

Write sentences using three of the words above that contain suffixes.

_____

_____

_____

PREVIEWING AND PREDICTING

Before reading a story, it can be helpful to study the title, illustrations, and subtitles. Look for clues that can help you predict what might happen in the story. Use information in the title, illustration, and subtitles to answer the following questions.

1. How does the title suggest that this story is a myth?

    _____

    _____

2. What can you predict about the story from reading the subtitles?

    _____

    _____

3. What clues about story events do you find in the picture?

    _____

    _____

DRAWING CONCLUSIONS

Before reading…

In northern Europe there once lived a hardy, seafaring people called Vikings, or Norsemen. They told of stories Odin, chief of the gods, who lived in the realm of Asgard. In this Norse myth, the mighty god Odin is called upon to make a great sacrifice.

ODIN'S QUEST FOR WISDOM

As chief of the gods, Odin often had to make tough decisions. His job required great knowledge and good judgment. Odin knew just where such wisdom could be found. He knew he must travel to Jotunheim, land of the giants. There, an aged giant named Mimir guarded a magical well. Its waters contained wisdom and understanding.

The mighty traveler began his pilgrimage by crossing a rainbow bridge. It took him out of Asgard—the splendid land of gods and dead heroes. What a fine figure Odin made! A hooded blue cloak dappled with gray enveloped him like a sky filled with clouds.

Odin's journey was long—but at last he reached Jotunheim. There he found the giant Mimir resting beside his well.

Odin stared into the bottomless depths of Mimir's magical well. Then he looked into the giant's eyes. He saw that they were as clear and deep as the water. "I come to drink from your well, Mimir," Odin said.

Mimir tugged at his long white beard and thought for a moment. "The water and its powers do not come free," he said at last. "The price is high." Mimir drew a cup of the clear water and held it out to Odin. "If you want to drink, you must leave me one of your eyes."

Odin did not bicker or bargain. He knew that no one can expect something for nothing. In order to get, one must give. Yes—even the gods had to work and struggle to gain what they desired! And Odin greatly desired the wisdom of the well. Without a moment's pause, the great god plucked out one eye and handed it to Mimir.

Do not pity Odin as a half-blind god. It was true that he could no longer see the outside world as clearly as he once had. But Odin now had a new kind of sight. Brilliant thoughts and ideas filled his head—a kind of knowledge known as *insight*.

For the most part, Odin was happy. For many, many years he showed good judgment in his decisions and ruled wisely. But the drink of Mimir's water had brought with it a greater understanding of the future—an ability to predict what was to be. Now Odin saw that all things must end. Even the gods would some day pass away. The drink from Mimir's well had forever changed Odin's appearance. He not only had but a single eye—but, from that day forth, he wore a sadder look.

COMPREHENSION

Draw a line to match each word on the left with its description.

1. **Odin**   a. land of giants

2. **Asgard**   b. land of gods and dead heroes

3. **Mimir**   c. chief of gods

4. **Jotunheim**   d. giant guardian of the well

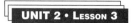

Write your answers on the lines.

5. Why did Odin journey to Jotunheim? _____

_____

6. What was Mimir's price for allowing Odin to drink from his well?

_____

7. In what way did the trip to Jotunheim make Odin happier?
   Why did it also make him sadder? _____

_____

_____

DRAWING CONCLUSIONS

As you read, you will often make decisions or form opinions by thinking about details and events in a story.

1. A reader could draw several conclusions based on the events in "Odin's Quest for Wisdom." Put a checkmark (✔) beside *two* reasonable conclusions.

   _____ As a god, Odin expected to be given everything he wanted.

   _____ Nothing worth having comes without cost.

   _____ Mimir and Odin secretly hated each other.

   _____ Everyone in Asgard loved and admired Odin.

   _____ Great knowledge and insight can bring some sadness.

2. Now use story details and events to form an opinion. Write your answer to the question on the lines.

   Do you think Odin was a good chief of gods? Why or why not?

   _____

   _____

VOCABULARY

Choose a word from the box that is a *synonym* (word with a similar meaning) for the **boldface** word in each sentence. Spell each word on the blanks after the sentence.

quest	pilgrimage	dappled	bicker	plucked	insight

1. Odin did not want to **argue** with Mimir,
   so he agreed to his terms.   __ __ __ __ __ __

2. Odin's **journey** to Jotunheim took
   him across the rainbow bridge.   __ __ __ __ __ __ __ __ __ __

3. Odin's blue cloak was **spotted** with flecks
   of gray like clouds in the sky.   __ __ __ __ __ __ __

4. The **search** for knowledge led Odin to
   Mimir's well.   __ __ __ __ __

5. After drinking from the well, Odin had
   new **understanding** about the present
   and the future.   __ __ __ __ __ __ __

6. Only after Odin had **snatched** out his eye
   was he allowed to drink the water.   __ __ __ __ __ __ __

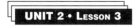

VISUALIZING

Use descriptive details from the myth to form a mental picture of Odin and
Mimir. Then, in the box below, sketch a scene or character from the story.
Label some of the items in your picture that are mentioned in the text.

ANTONYMS

First unscramble the words in the box. (The scrambled words are *antonyms*— words that mean the opposite—of words in the story.) Then cross out the incorrect word in each sentence and write the correct word on the line.

GOUHT _____	**GLON** _____
DEAG _____	**KECRIB** _____
TYMHIG _____	**TYPI** _____

1. Odin often had to make easy decisions. _____

2. Do not envy Odin as a half-blind god. _____

3. Odin did not agree with Mimir. _____

4. The weak traveler began his pilgrimage. _____

5. The youthful Mimir lived in Jotunheim. _____

6. Odin's journey was very short. _____

MAKING COMPARISONS

A Norse poet once wrote:

Moderately wise each one should be,
Not overwise, for a wise man's heart
Is seldom glad.

Explain these lines in your own words. Tell how they relate to what happened in "Odin's Quest for Wisdom."

_____

_____

_____

_____

PUTTING EVENTS IN ORDER

Before reading...

This story begins when mighty King Uther ruled England. Notice how it sets the stage for the reign of the legendary King Arthur.

THE SWORD IN THE STONE

King Uther of England fiercely loved a lady named Igraine. He was desperate to win her hand. Merlin the magician came to the king's aid. He promised to help the king in exchange for granting one wish. King Uther must promise to give his firstborn child to the magician— who would then raise the child as he chose.

King Uther was so stricken with love that he could not resist Merlin's offer. The bargain was made, and King Uther was married. When a son, Arthur, was born, Uther kept his pact. Merlin carried baby Arthur away. He gave him to an honorable knight named Sir Ector to raise. The magician did not tell Ector that the baby was a prince. Not long after, King Uther died. He left no heir to the throne but Arthur. But only Merlin knew about the young Arthur. Ambitious knights fought among themselves to claim the crown.

Meanwhile, Arthur grew up with Sir Ector and his son Kay. When Arthur had grown to a young man of 15, Merlin decided that the time was right to give England its king.

In a London churchyard, a huge stone mysteriously appeared. A steel anvil sat atop it, and a sword stuck straight through the anvil and into the stone. These words were written on the stone in golden letters: *Whoever pulls this sword from the stone is rightful King of England.*

Great contests were held to try to remove the sword. But one after another, ambitious nobles failed to move it so much as an inch.

On New Year's Day, Sir Ector decided to attend a jousting festival in London. His son, Sir Kay, and his foster son, Arthur, came with him.

"Alas!" cried Kay upon arriving at the joust. "I've left my sword at home." He turned to Arthur. "Could you go fetch it?"

Arthur went quickly, happy to do his brother a favor. But when he arrived home, he discovered the door was locked. He could not get in. Then he remembered seeing the sword in the stone. On his way back to the festival, Arthur stopped at the churchyard. Finding it empty, he grasped the sword's handle, easily pulled it from the stone, and took it to Kay.

Kay immediately recognized the magic sword. He claimed that *he* had pulled it from the stone. But the honorable Sir Ector suspected something was amiss. He led his two boys back to the churchyard. In this holy place, Kay had no choice but to speak the truth. He had to admit that Arthur had brought the sword to him.

By now a crowd had gathered. The throng demanded that Arthur be put to a test. Young Arthur pushed the sword back into the stone as easily as one would push a knife into butter. Then one after another, members of the crowd tried to pull it out. "I can't do it. It is stuck fast!" each man declared.

Ector brought his foster son forward. Arthur took hold of the sword and pulled it out smoothly. Then commoners and nobles fell on their knees. They bowed before Arthur, the true King of England.

COMPREHENSION

Circle the letter of the correct answer to each question.

1. Why was Arthur raised by Sir Ector?

   a. Sir Ector was Arthur's father.

   b. Merlin asked Ector to raise the boy.

   c. Ector was Arthur's uncle.

2. Why does Arthur first pull the sword from the stone?

   a. He wants to be named king.

   b. He wants to give the sword to Sir Kay.

   c. He wants to use the sword in a fight.

3. What does it prove when Arthur pulls the sword from the stone?

   a. He is the rightful King of England.

   b. He is the mightiest knight in the land.

   c. He is Merlin's true son.

VOCABULARY

The words in the box are often found in tales of knights and their times.
Write each word on the line next to its definition.

knight	honorable	heir	anvil	joust

1. _____: a competition with lances between two
knights on horseback

2. _____: someone who has the legal right to another's title when the other person dies

3. _____: worthy of respect; honest, just, and moral

4. _____: a man in the Middle Ages who has been granted a military rank of honor

5. _____: an iron block on which metal objects are hammered into shape

READING FOCUS: PUTTING EVENTS IN ORDER

The following events from "The Sword and the Stone" are listed out of sequence. On the blanks below, write the letters of the events according to the order in which they happened.

1. _____ 2. _____ 3. _____ 4. _____ 5. _____ 6. _____ 7. _____ 8. _____

a. Ector, Arthur, and Kay went to a festival in London.

b. Kay said he had pulled the sword from the stone.

c. The crowd honored Arthur as King of England.

d. Arthur pulled the sword from the stone and took it to Kay.

e. Merlin gave Arthur to Sir Ector to raise.

f. Kay sent Arthur home for his sword.

g. Arthur pushed the sword back into the stone.

h. Arthur pulled the sword from the stone a second time.

RECOGNIZING CAUSE AND EFFECT

To identify an *effect*, ask yourself *what* happened. To identify a *cause*, ask yourself *why* it happened. Fill in the missing part of the cause and effect relationships shown below.

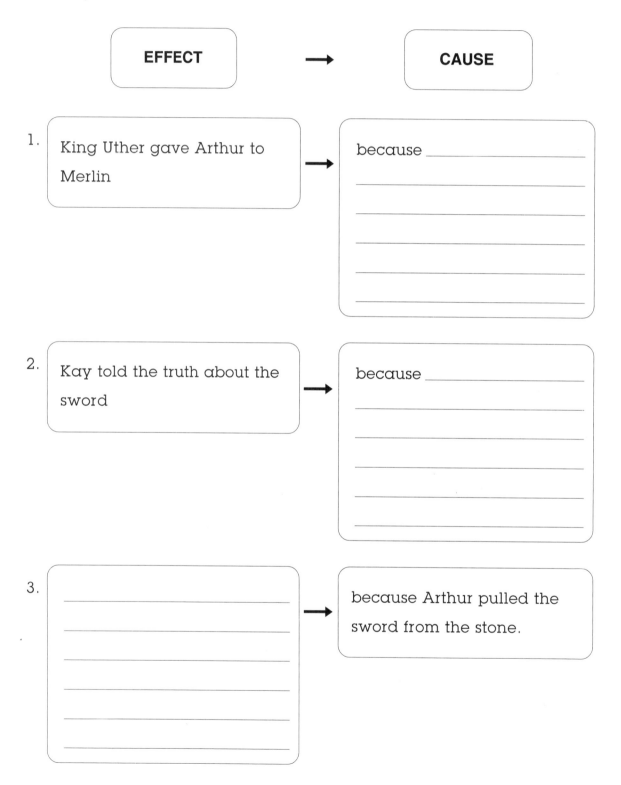

EFFECT → **CAUSE**

1. King Uther gave Arthur to Merlin → because _____

2. Kay told the truth about the sword → because _____

3. _____ because Arthur pulled the sword from the stone.

SYNONYMS

Synonyms are words that have similar meanings. In each group of words below, circle the synonym of the **boldface** word from the story. Then write a sentence using each word from the story.

1. **pact**   argument   agreement   war   ruling

2. **ambitious**   lazy   aspiring   weary   cruel

3. **fetch**   purchase   return   retrieve   swallow

4. **suspected**   guessed   hoped   hated   purchased

5. **throng**   individual   strap   commoner   crowd

6. _____

_____

7. _____

_____

8. _____

_____

9. _____

_____

10. _____

_____

MATCHING

Draw a line to match each story with its setting.

1. "The Myth of Daedalus and Icarus"
2. "How the Winds Began to Blow"
3. "Odin's Quest for Wisdom"
4. "The Sword in the Stone"

a. Asgard and Jotunheim
b. a village along the Yukon River
c. medieval England
d. the island of Crete

Who spoke the following lines? Match a character from the box with each line of dialogue. Write the name on the line.

| Icarus | Daedalus | Odin | Mimir | the doll | King Arthur | Merlin |

5. _____ "Keep a middle course! That is the way to stay safe."

6. _____ "Wind, blow hard sometimes. Blow softly sometimes."

7. _____ "The water and its powers do not come free."

8. _____ "Father is too old to enjoy this!"

MULTIPLE CHOICE

Circle the letter of the correct answer to each question.

1. What did it show about Icarus's character when he flew up toward the sun?
   a. He respects his father's greater experience and wisdom.
   b. He is reckless and thinks little of his father's advice.

2. Which of the following details help a reader figure out the setting of "How the Winds Began to Blow"?
   a. The woman and the man wished for a child of their own.
   b. The husband finds a snowy path on a frosty night.

3. Which detail in "Odin's Quest for Wisdom" helps a reader to conclude that Odin is a good ruler?
   a. Odin gives up his eye in exchange for a drink from the well of wisdom.
   b. The well of wisdom is guarded by the giant Mimir.

4. Which event happens at the end of "The Sword in the Stone"?
   a. Merlin gives Arthur to Sir Ector to raise.
   b. The people proclaim Arthur the true King of England.

FOLKTALES AND FABLES

LESSON 1: Understanding the Tall Tale: *The Steel-Driving Man*

LESSON 2: Recognizing Point of View: *Tales of Pecos Bill*

LESSON 3: Identifying Theme: *The Fable of the Discontented Fish*

LESSON 4: Comparing and Contrasting: *Two Trickster Tales*

When you complete this unit, you will be able to answer questions like these:

- *How is a fable different from a folktale?*

- *If we say a story has a "first-person narrator," what do we mean?*

- *In what kind of stories do writers use exaggeration?*

- *What words can clue you that an author is comparing or contrasting two different things?*

PRETEST

Write **T** or **F** to show whether you think each statement is *true* or *false*.

1. _____ In a tall tale you'll find very realistic characters and believable events.

2. _____ A tall tale is told in a casual tone, using the everyday speech of the region.

3. _____ The narrator tells the story from his or her point of view.

4. _____ The narrator is always a character in the story.

5. _____ The theme of a story usually expresses the point the author is making.

6. _____ When authors contrast two things, they point out how those things are similar.

Pretest answers: 1. F 2. T 3. T 4. F 5. T 6. F

UNDERSTANDING THE TALL TALE

Before reading . . .

One of America's most popular folk heroes is John Henry. The son of a slave, John Henry earned his fame as a railroad man. As such, he "pounded track" on the Chesapeake and Ohio Railroad in West Virginia. Stories are still told and songs are still sung about the man who was mightier than any machine.

THE STEEL-DRIVING MAN

They say that when John Henry was born, he cried his first cry and then reached for a hammer hanging on the cabin wall. They say he grasped that hammer and waved it like a rattle.

As John Henry grew, he toiled in the cotton fields—outworking every man, woman, and child. When the workday was done, other slave children played with toys. John Henry pounded his hammer.

The Civil War came, and John Henry watched trains carrying Southern soldiers north to battle. Only one thing fascinated the boy as much as his hammer. It was the railroad.

When the war was over and the slaves were freed, John Henry followed his dreams. "I'm off to work on the railroad," he told his daddy. "I'm going to be a steel-driving man! I was born with a hammer in my hand, and I'm bound to die with one, too!"

It didn't take John Henry long to find work. When he showed a railroad foreman how well he could swing a hammer, the man hired him on the spot.

Before long, everybody who knew about railroading knew about John Henry. He was the fellow who could hammer all day without rest. They say he could pound spikes so fast that the tracks caught fire!

In 1870, John Henry was working for the Chesapeake and Ohio Railroad. The C&O was drilling the Big Bend Tunnel through a mountain in West Virginia. Just about that time, a fellow was experimenting with a newfangled machine called a steam drill.

"I don't need any steam drill," the foreman exclaimed. "Nothing can go faster than John Henry!"

"Do you want to bet?" the other fellow asked.

That's how John Henry came to race the steam drill. He was bound to prove that he could dig a hole faster than any machine.

Race day arrived. John Henry was placed on the right-hand side. The steam drill was placed on the left. "Before I let that steam drill beat me, I'll *die* with this hammer in my hand!" John Henry roared.

Sounds of clanking and clanging filled the air as John Henry and the steam drill tore into the rock. John Henry pounded faster and faster until his arms were a blur of motion. By the time the race was over, a pool of sweat from John Henry's body nearly drowned several onlookers.

The judges were called over to measure the holes. The steam drill had bored 9 feet into the mountain. But John Henry had gone in 14 feet!

"I told you no machine could beat my man, John Henry!" cried the foreman. Everyone in the crowd cheered the steel-driving hero.

But John Henry was shaking his big head, trying to clear the whirring that rang in his ears. He stumbled and shook. Then, with a bang that shook the mountain, he fell to the ground. He was still clutching his hammer.

"I am bound to die with a hammer in my hand," John Henry had once predicted. And that's exactly what he did!

Before long, the steam drill took over all the steel-driving jobs. But folks haven't forgotten that it never did as good a job as John Henry!

COMPREHENSION

Fill in the blank to complete each sentence.

1. When John Henry was a child, he played with

   _____.

2. The railroad foreman quickly hired John Henry because _____

   _____.

3. While working on the railroad, John Henry raced against a

   _____.

4. _____ won the race.

5. After the race, John Henry _____.

UNDERSTANDING THE TALL TALE

The story of John Henry is the kind of folktale called a *tall tale*. Two characteristics of the tall tale are listed below. Match each characteristic with examples from "The Steel-Driving Man." Write the letters of the story example under the characteristic it illustrates.

CHARACTERISTICS

1. **casual, conversational tone**

   _____ _____ _____

2. **exaggerated abilities and impossible happenings**

   _____ _____ _____

EXAMPLES

a. They say that when . . .

b. Most folks think . . .

c. He grasped that hammer and waved it like a rattle.

d. newfangled machine

e. He could pound spikes so fast that the tracks would catch fire.

f. A pool of sweat from John Henry's body nearly drowned several onlookers.

FORESHADOWING

Sometimes an author gives hints or clues about what will happen later in the story. This is called *foreshadowing*. Think about foreshadowing as you answer each of the following questions.

1. Early in the tale, John Henry says something to his father that foreshadows the story's ending. What does John Henry say?

   _____

   _____

2. What happens to John Henry at the end of the tale? _____

   _____

   _____

VOCABULARY

Draw lines to match each vocabulary word with its *synonym* (word with the same meaning).

1. **spikes**   a. drilled

2. **foreman**   b. modern

3. **newfangled**   c. nails

4. **bored**   d. foresaw

5. **predicted**   e. boss

On the lines below, write two or three sentences *summarizing* what happened in the tale. Use at least two of the vocabulary words in your sentences.

_____

_____

_____

_____

_____

PUZZLER

Some story words give strong clues to *setting*. Unscramble the words below. The correctly written words give you clues about when and where the story takes place. As hints, use the letters provided.

1. LVCII RAW   C _ _ _ _   W _ _

2. TOCTNO DLEFIS   C _ _ _ _ _   F _ _ _ _ _

3. TORSNEUH   S _ _ _ _ _ _ _

4. EWTS IGIRIVAN   W _ _ _   V _ _ _ _ _ _ _

Write a sentence telling, in your own words, where and when this story takes place.

_____

_____

_____

WORDS WITH SOUND

Authors sometimes use words that *sound* like their meaning. This adds liveliness to their writing. Circle four words from the story that suggest sounds.

waved	swing	clanking
clanging	driving	buzzing
stumbled	bang	clutching

Now write a descriptive paragraph using at least two of the words you circled.

_____

_____

_____

_____

_____

_____

_____

_____

_____

ALPHABETICAL ORDER

On the lines below, write the story words in alphabetical order.

machine	steel	blur	hammer	onlookers
Southern	cabin	Civil	predicted	foreman

1. _____   6. _____

2. _____   7. _____

3. _____   8. _____

4. _____   9. _____

5. _____   10. _____

RECOGNIZING POINT OF VIEW

Before reading . . .

Pecos Bill was a remarkable cowboy. He was strong and brave and had a big heart, too. If anybody in the great Southwest needed help, Bill was there to lend a hand. You can take the word of someone who knew him well.

TALES OF PECOS BILL

You probably haven't heard of me, but you likely know of my pal, Pecos Bill. I'll start my tale with the day I first laid eyes on Bill. I'd finished running cattle into Texas and was riding along the banks of the Pecos River. I was chewing tobacco and minding my business when I came across a naked little boy. He was loping along the river bank on all fours. When he saw me, he snarled.

"Who in thunder are you?" I asked.

The boy looked at me curious-like, so I tossed him a plug of tobacco. He ate it, came closer, and started to sniff at me. Darned if he didn't seem to like my smell! I decided to make camp right then and there. The little boy curled up beside me like he meant to stay.

He was a smart young feller. After three days, he was talking to me in human-talk. Thinking back, he seemed to recollect the name of Bill. By and by, I figured out that he'd fallen from his ma and pa's wagon when it bumped along the rocky riverside.

There was just one thing Bill couldn't get straight. He thought he was a coyote. Seems he'd been adopted into a coyote pack and raised like a pup. "I *must* be a coyote!" Bill argued. "I've got fleas, and I howl at the moon."

"All Texans have fleas!" I told him. "If you were a coyote, you'd have a bushy tail."

Bill looked at his rear end and saw that I was right. He didn't have a tail! Now Bill was ready to leave the Pecos. He roped a mountain lion, straddled it, and rode off alongside me and my horse. From that time on I called my pal Pecos Bill.

When he grew up, Bill and I worked as hands at the Dusty Dipper Ranch. It was there Bill invented the ten-gallon hat and spurs. He rode horses no one else could break, and he taught cowboys to write songs.

Bill was a cowboy that folks could count on. He had a tender heart—and that's why he chased down a cyclone. When a drought swept the southwest prairie, crops dried up and farmers suffered plenty. Bill rode his horse, Widow Maker, around the dusty range looking for a way to help out. He spotted a cyclone and figured it held rain. So Bill lassoed that twister and climbed aboard. My pal rode the cyclone west to California. When he got there, he tightened his rope and squeezed out every drop of rain. Finally, that cyclone ran out of steam. That's when big Bill tumbled to the ground. His fall punched a big hole in the ground that folks later named Death Valley.

You may wonder what happened to Bill. Yep, you're right—you haven't seen him around these parts lately. I'm sorry to say my pal went to the big roundup in the sky. It happened when Bill and I were on a cattle drive in Colorado. We met a dude from back east who fancied himself a cowboy. He didn't know a rope from a rattlesnake! The fellow asked a zillion silly questions about cow punching. Bill couldn't stop laughing! Now you may think it's a sad end that Bill met—but to my thinking, it's the best way a fellow could go. Pecos Bill just laughed himself right to death.

COMPREHENSION

Write your answers in complete sentences.

1. Where did the narrator first meet up with Pecos Bill? What was Bill doing? _____

   _____

2. How did the narrator convince Bill that he wasn't a coyote?

   _____

3. How did Pecos Bill end a long dry spell in California? _____

   _____

4. How did Pecos Bill die? _____

   _____

RECOGNIZING POINT OF VIEW

Some stories are told by an outside narrator who is not part of the story. This type of story is told from the *third-person point of view*. A third-person narrator, for example, tells "The Steel-Driving Man"—the first tall tale in this unit.

Some stories are told from the *first-person point of view*. A first-person narrator is a character in the story. This narrator uses the words *I, me, my,* and *we* when telling the story.

Circle a letter to answer each question.

1. Who tells the "Tales of Pecos Bill"?

   a. a cowboy in the story who becomes a pal of Bill's

   b. an outside narrator who is not part of the story

2. From what point of view is the "Tales of Pecos Bill" told?

    a. third-person point   b. first-person point
        of view   of view

3. Which sentence reveals that the story is written from the first-person point of view?

    a. I'll start my tale with   b. Pecos Bill was the most
        the day I first laid eyes   famous cowboy who
        on Bill.   ever lived.

In each sentence below, circle the word that shows the sentence is told from the *first-person* point of view.

4. When he saw me, he snarled.

5. "All Texans have fleas!" I told him.

6. We worked together as hands at the Dusty Dipper Ranch.

To identify the point of view, write **first person** or **third person** next to each of the following sentences.

7. _____ "Who in thunder are you?" I asked.

8. _____ "Who in thunder are you?" the cowboy asked.

9. _____ The boy curled up beside the cowboy like he meant to stay.

10. _____ The boy curled up beside me like he meant to stay.

11. _____ We met a dude from back east who fancied himself a cowboy.

VOCABULARY: USING CONTEXT CLUES

What does the **boldface** vocabulary word in each sentence mean? Circle other words in the sentence that help you figure out its meaning. Then write a definition of the word on the line. Try to figure out the definition from context—but use a dictionary if you need help.

1. Thinking back, he seemed to **recollect** the name of Bill.

   DEFINITION: _____

2. He spotted a **cyclone** and figured it held rain. Bill lassoed that twister.

   DEFINITION: _____

3. Seems he'd been **adopted** into a coyote pack and raised like a pup.

   DEFINITION: _____

4. We met a **dude** from back east who fancied himself a cowboy.

   DEFINITION: _____

COMPOUND WORDS

A *compound word* is made up of two or more parts. Each part can stand on its own as a separate word. Using word parts from the box, complete each sentence with the correct compound word. Use the word's first letter as a clue. Hint: You will use some word parts more than once.

along	boy	cow	rattle	river	side	snake	south	west

1. The narrator discovered Bill loping on all fours along the

   *r*_____ .

2. Bill and the mountain lion traveled *a*_____ the narrator and his horse.

3. Bill rode the cyclone across America's S_____,
from Texas to California.

4. The dude wasn't smart enough to recognize a hissing, crawling
r_____.

5. Bill invented all sorts of c_____ gear, such as
spurs and the ten-gallon hat.

PUZZLER

Use the clues to help you complete the crossword puzzle.

ACROSS

2. the region where the narrator first met Bill

3. Bill rode this kind of storm to make rain.

5. California landmark Bill created when he fell (two words)

7. roping, riding, cattle-driving fellows

DOWN

1. wild animal of the prairies that raised Bill as its own

3. state where Bill met his end

4. what Bill fell out of when he was a child

6. long rope with a loop at the end; Bill used one to snag the cyclone

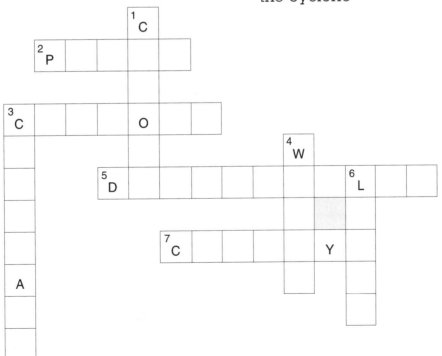

IDENTIFYING THEME

Before reading . . .

A *fable* is a folktale that points to a truth or teaches a lesson. Most fables have animal characters who talk and act like humans. Fables come from all parts of the world—but the lessons they teach are very similar. This African fable teaches a lesson about pride.

THE FABLE OF
THE DISCONTENTED FISH

Once there was a small, still pond. Smooth stones covered its bottom. Palm trees on its bank cast cool shadows on the blue waters. In the pond lived a colony of small, brightly colored fish. One fish was noticeably larger than the rest. He was not only longer and wider, but also much stronger. The big fish thought he was something special. "Do this," he bossed the other fish. "Do that! Get out of my way, short stuff. A big fellow like me needs fin-room!"

The little fish didn't like the big fish very much. "Let's ignore him," they'd say to one another. But a bully is hard to ignore. The little fish were forever being pushed and shoved about the pond.

There came a day when one little fish stood up for her rights. She challenged the big fish. "Since you're such great stuff," she said, "why don't you leave this little pond? Surely a fellow like you could make a splash in a more important place. Try the big river! There you could hang out with those who are as grand as you are!"

The big fish swam off. He circled slowly in a shady corner of the pond. The other fish could see that he was thinking. "Maybe the little gal has a point," the big fish pondered. "Why should I settle for the company of minnows when I could swim with the sharks? I was meant for greater things!"

So the big fish waited for the summer rains. When they came, the little pond would overflow its banks and floodwaters would meet the big river. Finally, in the midst of a downpour, the big fish left the only home he'd ever known. Swirling waters carried him into the river.

It was a different world indeed! The river rocks were large. The river weeds were tall. The current was swift and strong. "This is more like it!" the fish exclaimed, exploring his impressive new home.

Suddenly a big river fish swam by. He shouted, "Out of the way, little fish!" Then a whole school of big fish approached. They glared at him suspiciously. "Move on! This is our hunting ground!" they warned. They chased the smaller pond fish behind a clump of weeds. There he hid, frightened and unhappy. "Why did I come to this horrible place?" he wondered.

The pond fish remained in hiding until there were no strangers in sight. Then he headed upstream to where the floodwaters entered the river from the pond. Swimming there was hard. The swift current dashed him against the rocks again and again. Yet still, he struggled on.

At last the fish made it back to the pond. There he lay on the bottom rocks, his gills opening and closing as he fought for breath. The tiny fish swam by and stared. Finally, he gasped, "I'm so glad to be home! If I had known what the river was like, I'd never have left our pond!"

From that day forth, the big fish never spoke an unkind word to the smaller fish. He no longer complained about the little pond or wished for something grander. Indeed, the big fish was grateful for his world and the company of friends.

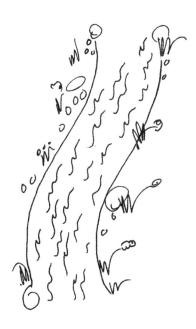

COMPREHENSION

Write **T** if the statement is *true* or **F** if the statement is *false*. Write **NI** for *no information* if the article does not provide that information.

1. _____ The small fish didn't like the big fish because he was a bully.

2. _____ The big fish wished he were smaller so he would fit in with the crowd.

3. _____ The big fish thought he was too grand for the little pond.

4. _____ The pond fish were mostly trout and guppies.

5. _____ The big pond fish found that life in the river was not as wonderful as he had expected.

6. _____ The river fish gave the pond fish a friendly welcome.

7. _____ In the river, the tables were turned, and the pond fish was the little guy.

8. _____ If the pond fish had stayed in the river longer, he would have learned how to get along.

9. _____ Once the pond fish returned to the pond, he was still discontented and unhappy.

10. _____ The trip to the river changed the big fish's attitude.

IDENTIFYING THEME

The point the writer is trying to make can be found in the story's *theme*. In a fable, the theme is called a *moral*. The moral teaches a lesson about life.

1. What lesson does "The Fable of the Discontented Fish" teach? Circle the letter of the best answer.

    a. Appreciate what you have.

    b. If you can't say something nice, don't say anything at all.

    c. Honesty is the best policy.

    d. Love of money is the root of all evil.

2. Stories often have more than one theme. Read each of the following morals. Tell how "The Fable of the Discontented Fish" teaches each lesson.

    a. **Too much pride can be a dangerous thing.** _____

    _____

    _____

    _____

    _____

    b. **The grass often seems greener on the other side of the fence.**

    _____

    _____

    _____

    _____

    c. **Look before you leap.** _____

    _____

    _____

    _____

SYNONYMS AND ANTONYMS

Read the vocabulary words. Choose a *synonym* (word with a similar meaning)
from the box to write in the second column. Then choose an *antonym* (word with
the opposite meaning) from the box to write in the third column.

dared	grand	pleaded	thug	unhappy
frowned	inferior	friend	satisfied	smiled

VOCABULARY WORD	SYNONYM	ANTONYM
1. bully	_____	_____
2. challenged	_____	_____
3. discontented	_____	_____
4. glared	_____	_____
5. impressive	_____	_____

DIALOGUE

When characters talk to each other, they are having a *dialogue*. The author
puts a character's words inside quotation marks. Read the following dialogue
from the fable. Then circle the character traits that each quotation reveals.

1. "Do this," the big fish bossed the other fish. "Do that! Get out of my
   way, short stuff. A big fellow like me needs fin-room!"

   THIS QUOTE SHOWS THE BIG FISH IS: pushy   conceited   sweet

   humble   generous   self-important

2. "Since you're such great stuff," said the little fish, "why don't you
   leave this little pond?"

   THIS QUOTE SHOWS THE LITTLE FISH IS: bold   impatient   meek

   angry   friendly   daring

3. "Move on! This is our hunting ground!" the river fish warned.

   THIS QUOTE SHOWS THE RIVER FISH ARE: unfriendly   hostile   generous

   neighborly   friendly   bossy

4. Finally the big fish gasped, "I'm so glad to be home! If I had known what the river was like, I'd never have left our pond!"

   THIS QUOTE SHOWS THE BIG FISH IS: arrogant   grateful   bossy

   appreciative   humble   cruel

Reread the words of the big pond fish in quotations one and four. Then, on the lines below, explain how the big fish's attitude changes from the beginning of the tale to its end.

_____

_____

_____

_____

_____

_____

SPELLING

Circle the correctly spelled word in each group.

1. shadey   shady   shaddy

2. noticeably   noticably   noticabally

3. horreble   horrable   horrible

4. minows   minnows   minnoes

5. suspiciously   suspisiously   sucspiciously

COMPARING AND CONTRASTING

Before reading . . .

Folktales in many parts of the world describe the adventures of *tricksters*. These clever characters figure out unusual ways to get what they want. Here are the adventures of two Native American tricksters. What do you think—would you call these characters heroes or rascals?

TWO TRICKSTER TALES

Rabbit Turns Trickster

When Bear met an enemy, he could strike out with sharp talons. Eagle could soar out of danger's reach. But when Rabbit felt threatened, he could only run for his life!

"It's not fair!" Rabbit complained to Master-of-Breath, the Life Controller. "The other animals have good ways to protect themselves."

"Do these tasks for me," Master-of-Breath said. "Then I will grant you a special power. But first, bring Rattlesnake to me."

Rabbit picked up a stick and went looking for Rattlesnake. He found him coiled and ready to strike. "Master-of-Breath wants to know how long you are, Rattlesnake," Rabbit said.

Rattlesnake was proud of his length. To show off, he stretched out in front of Rabbit. Rabbit quickly stuck his stick through the snake. Then he picked up the wriggling reptile and carried it back to Master-of-Breath.

"Well done," said the Master. "Now bring me a swarm of gnats."

Rabbit grabbed a bag. He called out to the King of the Gnats, "Master-of-Breath asked me to count the members of your throng."

The King of the Gnats was proud of his many followers. He was happy to have them counted. "Fly into this bag," Rabbit told the gnats. "I'll count each of you as you enter. The king flew in, followed by all the rest of the little bugs. Rabbit quickly tied up the bag and took it to the Master.

"I have done as you asked. Now may I have my special power?" asked Rabbit.

"You did these tasks with the powers you possess," Master-of-Breath replied. "You need no more. Go and use what you already have."

Coyote Outsmarts the Trader

Coyote watched settlers moving into the West. He saw how they took advantage of natives who already lived on the plains. "These newcomers think they are hot stuff," Coyote thought. "Someone should give them a taste of their own medicine!"

One day a certain trader bragged loudly. "Nobody gets the best of me!" he declared. "I'm the sharpest trader around!"

"There's someone who can outsmart you," folks warned the trader. They pointed him toward the trading post. There on the porch sat Coyote.

The trader strutted toward Coyote. "Hey!" he called. "I hear you're a clever dealer. Let's see you outsmart me!"

"I'd give it a try," Coyote said, "but I don't have my cheating tonic with me."

"What a miserable excuse!" said the trader. "Go get it then!"

"I live a long ways from here," Coyote said. "It would take me too long to walk home. But if you'll lend me your horse, I'll be happy to go."

The trader decided to call Coyote's bluff. "You can borrow my horse. Go get your cheating tonic!"

"Your horse seems a bit shy," Coyote said. "Why don't you lend me your clothes? The horse will think I'm you, and he won't be nervous."

The trader took off his clothes, and Coyote put them on. "Now, go fetch your cheating tonic," the fellow said, "—if there *is* such a thing!"

The trader, dressed only in his underwear, watched his horse, his clothes, and the crafty Coyote disappear across the plains.

COMPREHENSION

Write your answers in complete sentences.

1. What does Rabbit complain about to Master-of-Breath? _____

   _____

2. Master-of-Breath tells Rabbit to use the powers he already has. What powers do you think Rabbit has? _____

   _____

3. Why is Coyote anxious to trick the trader? _____

   _____

4. Does the trader really believe there is such a thing as "cheating tonic"? What makes you think so? _____

   _____

5. How does Coyote make a fool of the trader? _____

   _____

COMPARING AND CONTRASTING

Words such as *both, similarly, like,* and *also* are clues that a writer is making a *comparison* (telling how two things are alike). Words such as *but, different, in contrast,* and *on the other hand* are clues that a writer is showing a *contrast* (telling how things are different).

First, read the following paragraphs. Then fill in the blanks with words from the box. The first letter of each word has been provided as a clue. Finally, find and circle some of the clue words you learned about in the previous paragraph.

trickster	**human**	**coyote**	**rabbit**	**wits**	**clever**	**animal**

     Native American folklore from various regions presents different trickster characters. The first tale comes from the Southwest. It tells about a trickster _r_____ who outsmarts a rattlesnake and some gnats. In contrast, the second tale from the midwestern plains is about a _c_____ who gets the best of a trader.

     Both stories are _t_____ tales that tell about _c_____ characters who use their _w_____ to get what they want. Rabbit outsmarts _a_____ characters. Coyote, on the other hand, takes on a _h_____ and wins! Rabbit uses his slyness in hopes of gaining something for himself. But Coyote plays his trick for the pure joy of getting the best of a smart aleck.

UNDERSTANDING IDIOMS

An *idiom* is an expression that has taken on a different meaning from the usual meaning of the words. Read the following idioms from "Coyote Outsmarts the Trader." Circle a letter to show the expression's meaning in the tale.

1. "Someone should give them **a taste of their own medicine!**"

   a. They are sick and need medicine to get well.

   b. The cheaters should find out how it feels to be cheated.

2. "These newcomers think they are **hot stuff**," Coyote thought.

   a. Newcomers have trouble adjusting to the hot summers on the plains.

   b. The newcomers think they are smarter and wiser than the natives.

3. The trader decided to **call Coyote's bluff.**

   a. The trader wanted to catch Coyote in a lie.

   b. The trader wanted to name the town "Coyote's Bluff."

VOCABULARY

Use the vocabulary words from the box to complete the *analogies*. The second pair of words in each set should show the same relationship as the first pair. The first analogy has been done for you as an example.

coiled	gnat	strutted	swarm	talons	tonic

1. human : fingers

   eagle : _____*talons*_____

2. long : stretched

   round : _____

3. sheep : flock

   insects : _____

4. reptile : rattlesnake

   insect: _____

5. death : poison

   health : _____

6. talked : bragged

   walked : _____

PREFIXES

Add the prefix *un-* or *dis-* to the beginning of each **boldface** word. Write the new word to complete each sentence.

1. The rattlesnake **(coiled)** _____ and stretched out in front of Rabbit.

2. At first, Rabbit was **(aware)** _____ of his own special powers.

3. Master-of-Breath helped Rabbit **(cover)** _____ that he was very clever.

4. Rabbit **(tied)** _____ the bag, invited the gnats inside, and then tied it up again.

5. Coyote **(agreed)** _____ with the way the settlers treated the natives.

6. The trader should have been wise enough to **(trust)** _____ Coyote.

7. When Coyote mentioned his "cheating tonic," the trader looked at him with **(belief)** _____.

8. The trader **(dressed)** _____ and gave Coyote his clothes.

9. The trader watched crafty Coyote ride into the distance and **(appear)** _____.

MULTIPLE CHOICE

Circle the letter of the correct answer.

1. Which of the following is an "amazing" or "extraordinary" event typical of a tall tale? (You may circle more than one letter.)

   a. Pecos Bill tamed horses that were difficult to break.

   c. Pecos Bill roped and rode a cyclone.

   b. John Henry reached for a hammer the moment he was born.

   d. As a boy, John Henry was interested in trains.

2. What are two differences between "Tales of Pecos Bill" and "Two Trickster Tales"? (circle two letters)

   a. One story takes place in the present day, and the other takes place in the past.

   b. One story has a very formal tone, while the other is casual and conversational.

   c. One story has only human characters, while the other has animal characters.

   d. "Tales of Pecos Bill" is told from the first-person point of view. In contrast, "Two Trickster Tales" has a third-person narrator.

3. Which of the following is a theme of "The Fable of the Discontented Fish"?

   a. It's important to appreciate what you have.

   c. To do something well takes practice.

   b. Don't put off until tomorrow what you can do today.

   d. A fish can't live out of water.

4. Which of the following is a theme of the tale "Rabbit Turns Trickster" from "Two Trickster Tales"?

   a. Those who play tricks on others may end up being tricked themselves.

   c. Cheaters never prosper.

   b. Don't overlook the talents you possess.

   d. Honesty is the best policy.

POPULAR POETRY

LESSON 1: Using Descriptive Devices: *The Poet's Eye on Animals*

LESSON 2: Recognizing Author's Viewpoint and Purpose:
The Poet's View on War

LESSON 3: Reading a Monologue/Understanding Character:
Spoon River Anthology

LESSON 4: Recognizing Tone: *On the Light Side*

When you complete this unit, you will be able to answer questions like these:

■ *What are some descriptive devices that poets use to make an experience come alive for their readers?*

■ *What is a* monologue*?*

■ *How does a poet create* rhythm *in a poem?*

■ *How does a poet appeal to the reader's* senses*?*

PRETEST

Write **T** or **F** to show whether you think each statement is *true* or *false*.

1. _____ The description "Like a thunderbolt the eagle falls" is an example of a *simile*.

2. _____ The words "bow-wow" and "cock-a-doodle-doo" are examples of *personification*.

3. _____ Most poets present facts rather than their own opinions about a topic.

4. _____ A *monologue* is a conversation between two characters.

5. _____ Limericks have a lighthearted, humorous tone.

6. _____ When people say the opposite of what they really mean, it is called *irony*.

USING DESCRIPTIVE DEVICES

Before reading . . .

If you want to know about an eagle, you might turn to an encyclopedia or Internet article. You could find all sorts of facts and information. A look at the eagle through the poet's eye will help you appreciate the bird in a different way. Poetry can give you a deeper experience that involves your senses. It can spark an image of the eagle's power and majesty. As you read, notice how poets create word-pictures about creatures of the animal world.

THE POET'S EYE ON ANIMALS

The Eagle

He clasps the crag with crooked hands;
Close to the sun in lonely lands,
Ringed with the azure world, he stands.

The wrinkled sea beneath him crawls;
He watches from his mountain walls,
And like a thunderbolt he falls.

—Alfred, Lord Tennyson

Song

Hark, hark!
  Bow-wow.
The watch-dogs bark!
  Bow-wow.
Hark, hark! I hear
The strain of strutting chanticleer
Cry, "Cock-a doodle-doo!"

— William Shakespeare

A Narrow Fellow in the Grass

A narrow fellow in the grass
Occasionally rides;
You may have met him—did you not?
His notice sudden is.

The grass divides as with a comb,
A spotted shaft is seen;
And then it closes at your feet
And opens further on.

He likes a boggy acre,
A floor too cool for corn.
Yet when a child, and barefoot,
I more than once, at morn,

Have passed, I thought, a whip-lash
Unbraiding in the sun—
When, stooping to secure it,
It wrinkled, and was gone.

Several of nature's people
I know, and they know me;
I feel for them a feeling
Of cordiality;

But never met this fellow,
Attended or alone.
Without a tighter breathing
And zero at the bone.

—Emily Dickinson

Night Clouds

The white mares of the moon rush along the sky
Beating their golden hoofs upon the glass Heavens;
The white mares of the moon are all standing
   on their hind legs
Pawing at the green porcelain doors of the
   remote Heavens.
Fly, mares!
Strain your utmost
Scatter the milky dust of stars,
Or the tiger will leap upon you and destroy you
With one lick of his vermilion tongue.

—Amy Lowell

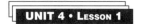

COMPREHENSION

Circle a letter to show how each sentence should be completed.

1. In "The Eagle," the poet describes

    a. an eagle perched on a cliff above the sea.

    b. an eagle soaring above a desert.

    c. a man with eyes as sharp as an eagle's.

2. In "Song," the poet helps the reader

    a. picture a dog and a rooster.

    b. understand how much he loves animals.

    c. hear the sounds of the dog and the rooster.

3. In the poem by Emily Dickinson, the "narrow fellow" is a

    a. spider.   b. snake.   c. kitten.

4. In "Night Clouds," the poet is describing

    a. horses.   b. clouds.   c. tigers.

VOCABULARY: "COLORFUL" WORDS

All four poets have chosen words that help readers see images in their minds. Reread each *italicized* word where it appears in the poem. Then circle the meaning of the word. Check a dictionary if you need help.

1. *azure* world ["The Eagle," line 3]

    Azure means (bright yellow / sky blue).

2. *wrinkled* sea ["The Eagle," line 4]

    The sea is (wavy and ridged / old and tired).

3. *strutting* chanticleer ["Song," line 6]

    The rooster is (limping / prancing).

4. *Unbraiding* in the sun ["A Narrow Fellow in the Grass," line 14]

    The snake is (stretching out to full length / curling up).

5. *vermilion* tongue ["Night Clouds," last line]

    The tiger's tongue is (pale pink / ruby red).

USING DESCRIPTIVE DEVICES

First, write a letter to match each descriptive device with its meaning.

1. _____ **simile**

    a. repetition of the beginning sounds of words

2. _____ **personification**

    b. words that sound like what they mean

3. _____ **onomatopoeia**

    c. giving a quality of a living thing to something that is not alive

4. _____ **alliteration**

    d. a comparison between two different things that uses the word *like* or *as*

Now, match the following lines with the device the poet is using. Write a letter by each number. (You may use a letter more than once.)

5. _____ He clasps the crag with crooked hands;

    a. **simile**

6. _____ Hark, hark! Bow-wow.

7. _____ The wrinkled sea beneath him crawls;

    b. **personification**

8. _____ And like a thunderbolt he [the eagle] falls.

9. _____ The strain of strutting chanticleer
Cry, "Cock-a-doddle-doo!"

    c. **onomatopoeia**

10. _____ The grass divides as with a comb,

    d. **alliteration**

SHOW YOUR UNDERSTANDING

Think of an animal you admire. Then choose two of the descriptive devices listed in the last activity. Write a sentence about the animal, using each descriptive device. Label each sentence with the descriptive device you used.

1. _____

_____

    DESCRIPTIVE DEVICE: _____

2. _____

_____

    DESCRIPTIVE DEVICE: _____

INTERPRETING POETRY

Because poets find new and different ways to say things, readers sometimes have to think hard about meaning. Notice the **boldface** word or phrase in each line from the poem. Circle a letter to show its meaning.

1. Ringed with **the azure world**, he stands. ("The Eagle")

   a. the sky and sea   b. the wind   c. the cliffs and rocks

2. Several of **nature's people**
   I know, and they know me; ("A Narrow Fellow in the Grass")

   a. farmers   b. creatures of the animal world   c. people who love the out-of-doors

3. **Without a tighter breathing**
   And zero at the bone. ("A Narrow Fellow in the Grass")

   a. happy feeling   b. sense of freedom   c. frightened feeling

4. **The white mares of the moon** rush along the sky ("Night Clouds")

   a. wild horses   b. night clouds   c. animals that hunt at night

RHYTHM AND SYLLABLES

Poets often use the same number of syllables in lines. Why? To create a *rhythm*—a flowing pattern of sounds. Count the syllables in each line below. Write the number of syllables in the blank before each line.

1. _____ A narrow fellow in the grass

   _____ Occasionally rides;

   _____ You may have met him—did you not?

   _____ His notice sudden is.

2. _____ He likes a boggy acre,

   _____ A floor too cool for corn.

   _____ Yet when a child, and barefoot,

   _____ I more than once, at morn,

3. _____ He clasps the crag with crooked hands;

   _____ Close to the sun in lonely lands,

   _____ Ringed with the azure world, he stands.

RHYMING WORDS

Lines of poetry often *rhyme*, or end with the same sounds. Go to the poem, and find a word that rhymes with each **boldface** word listed below. Then write another word that rhymes with these words.

POEM	WORD	RHYMING WORD FROM POEM	ANOTHER RHYMING WORD
1. "The Eagle"	**hands**	_____	_____
2. "The Eagle"	**crawls**	_____	_____
3. "Song"	**hark**	_____	_____
4. "A Narrow Fellow in the Grass"	**corn**	_____	_____
5. "A Narrow Fellow in the Grass"	**alone**	_____	_____

COMPARING AND CONTRASTING

Write **T** or **F** to tell whether each statement is *true* or *false*.

1. _____ "The Eagle" emphasizes the way an animal sounds while "Song" emphasizes the way animals look.

2. _____ The first three poems in this selection help readers picture animals. By contrast, "Night Clouds" uses the reader's knowledge of an animal to help them picture clouds.

3. _____ All the poems in this lesson rhyme.

4. _____ All the poems in this lesson mention animals.

5. _____ Because "A Narrow Fellow in the Grass" and "Song" are both told by first-person narrators, they use the word "I."

RECOGNIZING AUTHOR'S VIEWPOINT AND PURPOSE

Before reading . . .

Authors rarely make a *direct* statement of their reasons for writing. But readers can usually figure out the author's purpose. In this lesson, three poets express different viewpoints on war. Is war evil? Is war necessary? As you read, think about the poets' reasons for writing.

THE POET'S VIEW ON WAR

The Man He Killed
by *Thomas Hardy*

Had he and I but met
By some old ancient inn,
We should have sat us down to wet
Right many a nipperkin.[1]

But ranged as infantry,
And staring face to face,
I shot at him as he at me,
And killed him in his place.

I shot him dead because—
Because he was my foe,
Just so; my foe of course he was;
That's clear enough; although

He thought he'd 'list,[2] perhaps
Off-hand like—just as I—
Was out of work—had sold his traps[3]—
No other reason why.

Yes; quaint and curious war is!
You shoot a fellow down
You'd treat if met where any bar is,
Or help to half-a-crown.[4]

---

[1]*half-pint cup*   [2]*enlist*   [3]*the tools of one's trade*   [4]*an English coin*

90

Dragoon's[1] Song
by *George Henry Boker*

Clash, clash goes the saber against my steed's side,
Kling, kling go the rowels,[2] as onward I ride
And all my bright harness is living and speaks,
And under my horseshoes the frosty ground creaks;
I wave my buff glove to the girl whom I love,
Then join my dark squadron, and forward I move.

The foe, all secure, has lain down by his gun;
I'll open his eyelids before the bright sun.
I burst on his pickets;[3] they scatter and fly;
Too late they awaken,—'tis only to die.
Now the torch to their camp; I'll make it a lamp.
As back to my quarters so slowly I tramp.

Kiss, kiss me, my darling! Your lover is here,
Nay, kiss off the smoke-stains; keep back that bright tear;
To the low wailing fife and deep muffled drum,
With a bullet half through this bosom so true,
To die, as I ought, for my country and you.

---

[1]*member of a military unit*
of mounted troops

[2]*spurs*
[3]*soldiers acting as guards*

from *The Soldier*
by *Rupert Brooke*

If I should die, think only
  this of me;
That there's some corner of a
  foreign field
That is forever England.
  That there shall be
In that rich earth a richer
  dust concealed;

A dust whom England bore,
  shaped, made aware,
Gave, once, her flowers to love,
  her ways to roam,
A body of England's breathing
  English air,
Washed by the rivers, blest by
  suns of home.

COMPREHENSION

Write **T** or **F** to tell whether each statement is *true* or *false*.

1. _____ The poem, "The Man He Killed," is told by a soldier.

2. _____ The narrator of "The Man He Killed" enlisted in the army because he patriotically believed in his cause.

3. _____ The narrator of the first poem has strong feelings of ill will toward the man he killed.

4. _____ The poem, "Dragoon's Song," is told by a soldier.

5. _____ The soldier is part of a unit that rides horses.

6. _____ The narrator of "Dragoon's Song" and the narrator of "The Man He Killed" both kill an enemy soldier.

7. _____ The narrator of "The Soldier" is fighting a war against England.

8. _____ In "The Soldier," the narrator talks about proudly coming home from battle.

9. _____ In "The Soldier," the narrator is eager to die for his country in a foreign land.

10. _____ The narrator of "The Soldier" is angry that England's war could cost him his life.

UNDERSTANDING THE AUTHOR'S VIEWPOINT

Answer the questions in complete sentences.

1. In "The Man He Killed," what is the poet's attitude toward war?

_____

2. In "The Man He Killed," which stanza most clearly states the author's attitude toward war? Copy the first line of the stanza.

_____

3. In "Dragoon's Song," what is the poet's attitude toward war?

   _____

4. Copy a line from "Dragoon's Song" that expresses the poet's view.

   _____

5. The author of "The Soldier" also expresses a viewpoint about war. Is this view most like the one expressed in "The Man He Killed" or in "Dragoon's Song"? Explain your answer.

   _____

   _____

SUMMARIZING IDEAS

Each item below summarizes main ideas expressed in one of the poems. Write the name of the poem that expresses the ideas.

1. A soldier notes that war forces people to kill individuals they have no grudge against. His enemies might, in fact, be friends in another situation.

   NAME OF POEM: _____

2. A soldier thinks about dying in a foreign land. He asks to be remembered as a true Englishman who loved his country.

   NAME OF POEM: _____

3. In order to protect his country, this soldier is willing to kill or to give his life. He compares this feeling to dying to protect someone he loves.

   NAME OF POEM: _____

VOCABULARY PUZZLER

Use the clues to help you complete the crossword puzzle. Answers are words from the box.

roam	infantry	rowels	inn
quaint	saber	squadron	traps
tramp	pickets	concealed	

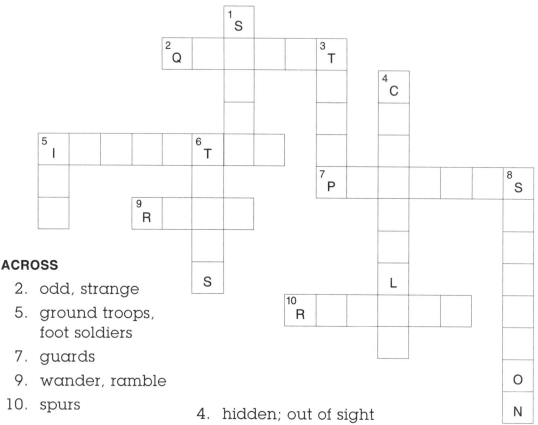

ACROSS

2. odd, strange
5. ground troops, foot soldiers
7. guards
9. wander, ramble
10. spurs
4. hidden; out of sight
5. a lodging or tavern
6. tools of a trade
8. group of soldiers in a military unit

DOWN

1. sword
3. march

APPEALING TO THE SENSES

Read each of the following lines from "Dragoon's Song." Circle the *sense* that the poet appeals to in each description. (You may circle more than one sense.)

1. *Clash, clash goes the saber against my steed's side,*

    taste   sight   sound   feeling   smell

2. *Kling, kling go the rowels, as onward I ride*

    taste   sight   sound   feeling   smell

3. *And under my horseshoes the frosty ground creaks.*

   taste   sight   sound   feeling   smell

4. *I wave my buff glove to the girl whom I love,*

   taste   sight   sound   feeling   smell

ANTONYMS

Read each line from the poem. Then underline the *antonym* (word with the
opposite meaning) of the **boldface** word.

1. I shot him dead because—
   Because he was my **foe**,   (enemy / friend / opponent)

2. I burst on his pickets; they **scatter** and fly;   (gather / divide / sing)

3. To the low **wailing** fife and
   deep muffled drum   (laughing / crying / loud)

4. That there's some corner of a **foreign** field
   That is forever England.   (far-off / native / unfamiliar)

RECOGNIZING AUTHOR'S PURPOSE

Choose one of the three poems from this lesson and write the title on the line.
Then, in the box below, draw a poster that has the same purpose as the poem.
(For example, a poster calling for peace rather than war; or, a poster urging
patriotic citizens to enlist in the armed forces.)

POEM TITLE: _____

READING A MONOLOGUE/ UNDERSTANDING CHARACTER

Before reading . . .

Have you ever visited a cemetery or looked at a picture of one? Did you wonder about the lives of those who lay buried there? In this excerpt from *Spoon River Anthology,* Edgar Lee Masters gives voices to the dead. You are about to meet a few of the people buried in the Spoon River cemetery. As you read, notice what each remembers and regrets about life.

SPOON RIVER ANTHOLOGY

Lois Spears

Here lies the body of Lois Spears,
Born Lois Fluke, daughter of
  Willard Fluke,
Wife of Cyrus Spears,
Mother of Myrtle and Virgil Spears,
Children with clear eyes and
  sound limbs—
(I was born blind).
I was the happiest of women
As wife, mother and housekeeper,
Caring for my loved ones,
And making my home
A place of order and bounteous
  hospitality;
For I went about the rooms,
And about the garden
With an instinct as sure as sight,
As though there were eyes in my
  fingertips—
Glory to God in the highest.

Cooney Potter

I inherited forty acres from my
  Father
And, by working my wife, my two
  sons and two daughters
From dawn to dusk, I acquired
A thousand acres. But not content,
Wishing to own two thousand
  acres,
I bustled through the years with
  axe and plow,
Toiling, denying myself, my wife,
  my sons, my daughters.
Squire Higbee wrongs me to say
That I died from smoking Red
  Eagle cigars.
Eating hot pie and gulping coffee
During the scorching hours of
  harvest time
Brought me here ere I had reached
  my sixtieth year.

Josiah Tompkins

I was well known and much
    beloved
And rich, as fortunes are
    reckoned
In Spoon River, where I had
    lived and worked.
That was the home for me,
Though all my children had
    flown afar—
Which is the way of Nature—
    all but one.
The boy, who was the baby,
    stayed at home,
To be my help in my failing
    years
And the solace of his mother.
But I grew weaker, as he grew
    stronger,
And he quarreled with me
    about the business,
And his wife said I was a
    hindrance to it;
And he won his mother to see
    as he did,
Till they tore me up to be
    transplanted
With them to her girlhood home
    in Missouri.
And so much of my fortune was
    gone at last,
Though I made the will just as
    he drew it,
He profited little by it.

Lucinda Matlock

I went to the dances at Chandlerville,
And played snap-out at Winchester.
One time we changed partners,
Driving home in the moonlight of
    middle June,
And then I found Davis.
We were married and lived together
    for seventy years,
Enjoying, working, raising the twelve
    children,
Eight of whom we lost
Ere I had reached the age of sixty.
I spun, I wove, I kept the house,
    I nursed the sick,
I made the garden, and for holiday
Rambled over the fields where sang
    the larks,
And by Spoon River gathering many
    a shell,
And many a flower and medicinal
    weed—
Shouting to the wooded hills, singing
    to the green valleys.
At ninety-six I had lived enough,
    that is all,
And passed to a sweet repose.
What is this I hear of sorrow and
    weariness,
Anger, discontent, and drooping
    hopes?
Degenerate sons and daughters,
Life is too strong for you—
It takes life to love Life.

COMPREHENSION

Answer each question on the lines.

1. What physical handicap did Lois Spears suffer in life?

   _____

2. Did Lois Spears lead a happy or unhappy life? _____

3. What things gave joy and meaning to Lois Spears' life?

   _____

4. During his life, how did Cooney Potter spend most of his time?

   _____

5. How does Cooney Potter *feel* about the way he spent his life?

   _____

6. How did the people of Spoon River think of Josiah Tompkins?

   _____

7. What happened to Josiah's wealth?

   _____

8. How long were Lucinda Matlock and her
   husband Davis married?   _____

9. How many children did they have? _____

10. How old was Lucinda when she died? _____

READING A MONOLOGUE

In a *monologue*, one person speaks as if talking to someone else. The poems in this lesson are monologues spoken by dead men and women who lay buried in the Spoon River cemetery. Their words can help you understand their personalities and lives.

Write a statement summarizing the life of each character. The first one has been done as an example.

1. **Lois Spears:** *Lois Spears was contented and fulfilled in life.*

   LINE FROM POEM: *"I was the happiest of women/As wife, mother and housekeeper."*

2. **Cooney Potter:** _____

   _____

   LINE FROM POEM: _____

   _____

3. **Josiah Tompkins:** _____

   _____

   LINE FROM POEM: _____

   _____

4. **Lucinda Matlock:** _____

   _____

   LINE FROM POEM: _____

   _____

VOCABULARY

Synonyms are words with the same or nearly the same meaning. Write the words in the poems that are *synonyms* of the **boldface** words.

"Lois Spears"

1. In line 11, which word means **generosity**? _____

2. In line 14, which word means **sense**? _____

"Cooney Potter"

3. In line 7, which word means **laboring**? _____

4. In line 11, which word means **sweltering**? _____

"Josiah Tompkins"

5. In line 9, which word means **comfort**? _____

6. In line 12, which word means **obstacle**? _____

7. In line 14, which word means **relocated**? _____

"Lucinda Matlock"

8. In line 12, which word means **wandered**? _____

9. In line 17, which word means **rest**? _____

10. In line 20, which word means **wicked**? _____

COMPARING CHARACTERS

Write your answers on the lines.

1. All four of the characters recall an unhappy fact they faced during their lives. Describe a problem that each one faced.

   Lois Spears: _____

   Cooney Potter: _____

Josiah Tompkins: _____

Lucinda Matlock: _____

2. Which two characters seem to have the most regrets

   about their lives? _____

3. Which two characters focus on the good rather than

   bad parts of life? _____

SUFFIXES

Add the correct *suffix* (word ending) from the box to each word in parentheses.
Write the new word on the line. Hint: You will use one suffix twice.

-al	-ance	-est	-eth	-hood	-ing	-ness

1. I was the **(happy)** _____ of women.

2. Eating hot pie and gulping coffee / During the scorching

   hours of harvest time/ Brought me here ere I had reached

   my **(sixty)** _____ year.

3. The boy, who was the baby, stayed at home, / To be my

   help in my **(fail)** _____ years.

4. And he quarreled with me about the **(busy)** _____ /

   And his wife said I was a **(hinder)** _____ to it.

5. Till they tore me up to be transplanted / With them to her

   (girl) _____ home in Missouri.

6. I rambled over the fields . . . and by Spoon River . . .

   gathering many a shell / And many a flower and

   (medicine) _____ weed.

7. What is this I hear of sorrow and **(weary)** _____ , /

   Anger, discontent, and drooping hopes?

RECOGNIZING TONE

Before reading . . .

Unusual characters, surprise endings, silly words, and a little teasing can all add humor to writing. The poems in this lesson are meant to amuse you. Although these poems are "on the light side," they still offer good reading—and, often, a bit of wisdom. Enjoy yourself!

ON THE LIGHT SIDE

Earth
by *John Hall Wheelock*

"A planet doesn't explode of itself," said dryly
The Martian astronomer, gazing off into the air—
"That they were able to do it is proof that highly
Intelligent beings must have been living there."

A Pocketful of Limericks
author: *anonymous*

There was a young lady of Lynn
Who was so uncommonly thin
    That when she essayed
    To drink lemonade
She slipped through the straw and fell in.

There was a young man who said, "Why
Can't I look in my ear with my eye?
    If I put my mind to it,
    I'm sure I can do it.
You never can tell till you try."

There was a young fellow of Perth
Who was born on the day of his birth;
    He was married, they say,
    On his wife's wedding day,
And he died when he quitted the earth.

Fable

by *Ralph Waldo Emerson*

The mountain and the squirrel
Had a quarrel,
And the former called the latter
  "Little Prig";
Bun* replied, "You are doubtless
  very big;
But all sorts of things and weather
Must be taken in together,
To make up a year
And a sphere.
And I think it no disgrace

To occupy my place.
If I'm not so large as you,
You are not so small as I,
And not half so spry.
I'll not deny you make
A very pretty squirrel track;
Talents differ; all is well and
  wisely put;
If I cannot carry forests on
  my back,
Neither can you crack a nut."

*nickname for the squirrel

Jabberwocky

by *Lewis Carroll*

'Twas brillig, and the slithy toves
  Did gyre and gimble in the wabe:
All mimsy were the borogoves,
  And the mome raths outgrabe.

"Beware the Jabberwock, my son!
  The jaws that bite, the claws
  that catch!
Beware the Jubjub bird, and shun
  The frumious Bandersnatch!"

He took his vorpal sword in hand;
  Long time the manxome foe
  he sought—
So rested he by the Tumtum tree,
  And stood a while in thought.

And, as in uffish thought he stood,
  The Jabberwock, with eyes
  of flame,
Came whiffling through the tulgey
wood,
  And burbled as it came.

One, two! One, two! And through
and through
  The vorpal blade went
  snicker-snack!
He left it dead, and with
its head
He went galumphing back.

"And hast thou slain the
Jabberwock?
  Come to my arms, my
  beamish boy!
O frabjous day! Callooh! Callay!"
  He chortled in his joy.

'Twas brillig, and the slithy
toves
  Did gyre and gimble in
  the wabe:
All mimsy were the
borogoves
  And the mome raths
  outgrabe.

COMPREHENSION

Write your answers on the lines.

"Earth"

1. What happened to the planet Earth? _____

2. What does the poem suggest caused the event? _____
   _____

Limericks

3. What problem did the young lady in the first limerick have?
   _____

4. What impossible task did the young man in the second
   limerick attempt to do? _____

"Fable"

5. Who are the two characters in this poem?
   _____

6. What character does most of the talking? _____

"Jabberwocky"

7. Although "Jabberwocky" has a lot of nonsense words, it tells a story.
   What do you think the story is about? _____
   _____
   _____

8. What real words in the poem give you clues to the story's plot?
   _____
   _____

RECOGNIZING TONE

You may have heard someone say, "I don't like the *tone* of his voice!" People often speak with an expression and manner that reflects an *attitude*. An author's style of writing can reflect attitude, too. Circle three words in the box that best describe the *tone* of these poems.

serious	**sorrowful**	**humorous**	**light**	**dark**
playful	**grim**	**insulting**	**sympathetic**	

IRONY

We say a writer is using *irony* when there is a clear difference between what is said and what is really meant. Imagine someone slipping on a banana peel and falling. "Well, that was fun!" the person says. Of course, the experience was not fun at all. Just the opposite! The speaker used irony to make a point.

1. Imagine that you have just returned from vacation. It rained. Your car had a flat tire. You got stung by bees. Write a sentence or two describing your trip. Use irony to make your point.

   _____

   _____

2. Explain how the poet uses irony in the last two lines of "Earth."

   _____

   _____

LOOKING AT LIMERICKS AND FABLES

Reread the "Pocketful of Limericks." Then decide if these statements about limericks are *true* or *false*. Write **T** or **F** beside each item.

1. _____ A limerick has five lines.

2. _____ Lines 1, 2, and 5 rhyme.

3. _____ Lines 1 and 3 rhyme.

4. _____ Lines 3 and 4 each have eight syllables.

5. _____ Lines 1, 2, and 5 each have eight syllables.

6. _____ The tone of a limerick is usually humorous.

Reread "Fable." Then decide whether each statement about fables is *true* or *false*. Write **T** or **F** beside each item.

7. _____ A fable tells a story.

8. _____ The characters in a fable are usually human beings.

9. _____ A fable usually ends stating a lesson or moral.

10. _____ Nonhuman characters in a fable act and talk like humans.

RHYMING

Add the missing words in each limerick. Make sure your word rhymes with the last word in the first line.

1. There once was a fellow named Blaine

   Who decided to build his own _____.

   He used cardboard and glue,

   Then flew into the blue,

   And never was heard from _____.

Remember "The Myth of Daedalus and Icarus" as you supply these rhyming words:

2. Young Icarus was a bold lad

   Whose fate, I'm afraid, was quite _____.

   He soared toward the sun,

   Just looking for fun.

   The boy should have heeded his _____.

VOCABULARY PUZZLER

Unscramble words from the poems that match the definitions. Some letters are given as clues. Another clue tells you where the word appears in the lesson.

1. scientist who studies planets, stars, suns, moons ("Earth," line 2)

   TOORSARMEN   __ _S_ __ __ __ _N_ __ __ __ __

2. tried, attempted (limerick #1, line 3)

   EDSASEY   __ _S_ __ __ _Y_ __ __

3. a person whose name is not known (author of limericks)

   NYMONASUO   __ _N_ __ _N_ __ __ __ __ __

4. planet, world ("Fable," line 8)

   PSHREE   _S_ __ __ __ _R_ __

5. dishonor, shame ("Fable," line 9)

   CIGARSED   __ __ __ _G_ __ __ _C_ __

6. laughed, chuckled gleefully ("Jabberwocky," verse 6, line 4)

   HERTCOLD   __ _H_ __ _R_ __ __ __ __

CLUES TO UNDERSTANDING

Try to figure out the meaning of some of the nonsense words in "Jabberwocky." Use context clues for help, and think about how the *sounds* of the words suggest a meaning. Then, rewrite the first stanza of "Jabberwocky." Replace the following nonsense words with real words: *brillig, slithy, toves, gyre, gimble, wabe, mimsy, borogoves, mome, raths, outgrabe.*

_____

_____

_____

_____

—— REVIEW ——

MATCHING

Match each term on the left with its meaning on the right. Write a letter by each number.

1. _____ **simile**

2. _____ **personification**

3. _____ **onomatopoeia**

4. _____ **alliteration**

5. _____ **monologue**

6. _____ **fable**

7. _____ **limerick**

8. _____ **tone**

9. _____ **irony**

a. a simple story having a lesson or moral

b. comment in which there is a difference between what is said and what is meant

c. giving the quality of a living thing to something not alive

d. comparison between different things, using the word *like* or *as*

e. five-line humorous verse with regular rhyme and rhythm

f. repetition of beginning sounds of words

g. words having a meaning that is a sound

h. writing style that reflects an author's attitude

i. passage in which one person speaks as if talking to someone else

MULTIPLE CHOICE

Circle the letter of the correct answer.

1. Which of the following lines is a *simile*?

   a. The watch-dogs bark!   c. The grass divides as with a comb.

   b. Fly, mares!   d. He watches from his mountain walls.

2. In which of the following does the poet use *personification*?

   a. The wrinkled sea beneath him crawls   c. A floor too cool for corn

   b. And like a thunderbolt he falls.   d. Hark, hark!

GLOSSARY OF READING TERMS

adapted rewritten to be made shorter or easier to read

alliteration repetition of the initial sound in two or more words; a poetic device

analyze to identify and examine the separate parts of a whole

author's purpose the writer's specific goal or reason for writing a particular book, article, etc.

categorize to divide into main subjects or groups

cause a happening or situation that makes something else happen as a result

classify to organize according to some similarity

compare to make note of how two or more things are alike

compound word a word made by combining two or more smaller words

conclusion the end or last part of a novel, article, etc.

context clues the words in a sentence just before and after an unfamiliar word or phrase. Context clues help to make clear what the unfamiliar word means.

contrast to make note of how two or more things are different from one another

describe to tell or write about something or someone in detail in order to help the reader or listener create a mental image

details bits of information or description that support the main idea and make it clearer

dialogue lines spoken by characters in a story or play

discuss to talk or write about a topic, giving various opinions and ideas

effect the reaction or impact that occurs as a result of a cause

elements the essential parts or components of a whole

excerpt section quoted from a book, article, etc.

fact something that actually happened or is really true

fiction literary work in which the plot and characters are imagined by the author

figurative language colorful, nonliteral use of words and phrases to achieve a dramatic effect

generalize to form a general rule or idea after considering particular facts

graphs charts or diagrams that visually present changes in something or the relationship between two or more changing things

homonyms words pronounced alike but having different meanings and usually different spellings

identify to name or point out; to distinguish someone or something from others

image idea, impression; a picture in the mind

inference conclusion arrived at by careful reasoning

interpret to explain the meaning of; to figure out in one's own way

judgment a decision made after weighing various facts

literature the entire body of written work including fiction, nonfiction, drama, poetry, etc.

locate find; tell where something is

main idea the point or central thought in a written work or part of a work

multiple-meaning words lookalike words that have different meanings in different contexts

nonfiction writing about the real world, real people, actual events, etc.

objective reflecting what is actual or real; expressed without bias or opinion

order items arranged or sequenced in a certain way, such as alphabetical order or order of importance

organize to put in place according to a system

outcome the result; the way that something turns out

parts of speech grammatical classifications of eight word types: adjective, adverb, conjunction, interjection, noun, preposition, pronoun, or verb

passage section of a written work

plot the chain of events in a story that leads to the story's outcome

plural word form showing more than one person, place, or thing

point of view the position from which something is observed or told; when a character tells the story, *first person* point of view is used; an author who tells the story in his own voice is using *third person* point of view.

predict to foretell what you think will happen in the future

prefix group of letters added at the beginning of a word to change the word's meaning or function

recall to remember or bring back to mind

refer to speak of something or call attention to it

relationship a connection of some kind between two or more persons, things, events, etc.

scan to glance at something or look over it quickly

sequence items in order; succession; one thing following another

singular word form naming just one person, place, or thing

subjective reflecting personal ideas, opinions, or experiences

suffix group of letters added at the end of a word that changes the word's meaning or function

symbol a concrete object used to represent an abstract idea

table an orderly, graphic arrangement of facts, figures, etc.

tense verb form that shows the time of the action, such as past, present, or future

term word or phrase with a special meaning in a certain field of study such as art, history, etc.

tone the feeling given by the author's choice of language

vocabulary all the words of a language